8512856
21-3760

/

Advance praise for
INVESTING IN IPOs
by Tom Taulli

SELECTED BY MONEY BOOK CLUB

"The Internet and other technologies are providing a sea of new opportunities for individual investors. . . . **THIS INFORMATIVE BOOK MAKES IT POSSIBLE FOR INVESTORS TO SIZE UP THE QUALITY AND GROWTH POTENTIAL OF THE IPOS THEY ARE INTERESTED IN**. I recommend reading *Investing in IPOs* by Tom Taulli before you start buying."

ANDREW D. KLEIN
Founder & Chief Strategist, Wit Capital Corporation

"IPOs are one of the stock market's biggest attractions, but scarce information is available about the process. . . . Tom Taulli gets inside the how-to and what-for of IPOs, **GIVING INVESTORS FROM ALL WALKS OF LIFE AN INSIDE LOOK AT HOW THEY REALLY WORK—CRUCIAL INFORMATION IN THE NEW INTERNET INVESTMENT ERA.**"

STEVE HARMON
Vice President, Business Development, Senior Investment Analyst, Mecklermedia, The Internet Media Company
Author of *The Internet Stock Report*

"**THIS BOOK OFFERS AN 'IPO MBA' FOR EVERYONE**—from novice to seasoned investor. Its easy-to-read format contains dozens of real-life examples that provide a much-needed user's manual for the world of IPOs."

FRANCIS GASKINS
Editor, *Gaskins IPO Desktop*

"**FINALLY, A BOOK THAT UNVEILS FOR INDIVIDUAL INVESTORS THE ONCE PROPRIETARY WORLD OF INITIAL PUBLIC OFFERINGS.** This book clearly explains how to uncover and investigate winning companies as they first become public.

Tom Taulli uses his considerable experience to bring to light the great potential that exists for investing, on-line and off, in today's growing companies."

DREW FIELD
Partner, Drew Field/Direct Public Offerings

"Tom Taulli has done an exceptional job of demystifying IPOs for investors with all levels of expertise. **THIS BOOK IS LONG OVERDUE!**"

JOHN E. FITZGIBBON, JR.
Editor, *IPO Reporter*

"*Investing in IPOs* by Tom Taulli is an invaluable guide for anyone participating in the frenetic world of IPOs. **THIS BOOK IS A GREAT INVESTMENT!**"

JAY SEARS
Vice President, Marketing & Business Development, *EDGAR Online,* Cybernet Data Systems, Inc.

"Tom Taulli has written **A COMPREHENSIVE AND INVALUABLE BOOK** on investing in initial public offerings for the individual investor. Not only does Taulli explain the IPO process from the beginning to end, but he also includes valuable information on how to access free research on the Internet, read a prospectus, and understand IPO risk factors."

LINDA R. KILLIAN
Principal, Renaissance Capital Corporation

"Tom Taulli has written the essential guide for investors who are puzzled by what IPOs are and how they work. The best investment strategies, the potential risks, and knowing when to get out once an IPO has fizzled—it's all here. . . . **YOU'D BE FOOLISH TO ENTER THE IPO MARKET WITHOUT READING THIS BOOK FIRST.**"

DAVID B. BATSTONE
Editor-at-Large, *Business 2.0*

Investing In
IPOs

BLOOMBERG PERSONAL BOOKSHELF

Investing In
IPOs

New Paths to Profit with Initial Public Offerings

TOM TAULLI

BLOOMBERG PRESS

PRINCETON

SIMSBURY PUBLIC LIBRARY
725 HOPMEADOW STREET
SIMSBURY, CT 06070

Books are available for bulk purchases at special discounts. Special editions or book excerpts can also be created to specifications. For information, please write: Special Markets Department, Bloomberg Press.

BLOOMBERG, BLOOMBERG NEWS, BLOOMBERG FINANCIAL MARKETS, OPEN BLOOMBERG, BLOOMBERG PERSONAL FINANCE, THE BLOOMBERG FORUM, COMPANY CONNECTION, COMPANY CONNEX, BLOOMBERG PRESS, BLOOMBERG PROFESSIONAL LIBRARY, BLOOMBERG PERSONAL BOOKSHELF, and BLOOMBERG SMALL BUSINESS are trademarks and service marks of Bloomberg L.P. All rights reserved.

First edition published 1999
1 3 5 7 9 10 8 6 4 2

Taulli, Tom, 1968–
    Investing in IPOs: New paths to profit with initial public offerings / Tom Taulli. –
    1st ed.
    Foreword by Steve Harmon
        p. cm. - - (Bloomberg personal bookshelf)
    Includes bibliographical references and index.
    ISBN 1-57660-067-X (alk. paper)
    1. Going public (Securities) 2. Investments. I. Title. II. Title: IPOs III. Series.
    HG4028.S7 T38 1999
    332.63'22 - - dc21
                                                    98-50315
                                                        CIP

Acquired and edited by Jacqueline R. Murphy
Book design by Don Morris Design

To my parents,
Tom and Anne Taulli,
who allowed me to
pursue my crazy ideas.

FOREWORD
by Steve Harmon **xiii**

INTRODUCTION 1

PART I
Introducing IPOs **10**

CHAPTER 1
IPO Basics
Introducing initial public offerings **12**

CHAPTER 2
The IPO Process
*A step-by-step tour—from number crunching
to the effective date* **28**

PART II
IPOs for Investors **42**

CHAPTER 3
Finding the Best IPO Information
*The most reliable IPO intelligence including
Web sites, newsletters, and magazines* **44**

CHAPTER 4
Making Sense of the Prospectus
*Decoding the fine print: how to size up past
performance and future prospects* **62**

CHAPTER 5
Risk Factors
A checklist of warning signs and red flags **80**

CHAPTER 6
IPO Investment Strategies
*Simple, commonsense guidelines and
more sophisticated techniques* **92**

PART III
Important IPO Sectors **104**

CHAPTER 7
Technology IPOs
*Prospecting for high-tech winners: Internet,
software, and telecom stocks* **106**

CHAPTER 8
Biotech IPOs
*Decoding a major market force of the future
and understanding its risks* **120**

CHAPTER 9
Finance Sector IPOs
*Banking, brokerage, mutual fund, and
insurance industry offerings* **134**

CHAPTER 10
Retail Sector IPOs
Spotting the lasting trends in the market **148**

CHAPTER 11
Foreign IPOs
Profiting from growth on a global scale **156**

PART IV

Other IPO Investments 168

C H A P T E R   1 2
IPO Mutual Funds
*Spotting funds that invest the most and best
in initial public offerings*   **170**

C H A P T E R   1 3
Virtual IPOs
*On-line pioneering efforts from
investment community entrepreneurs*   **180**

C H A P T E R   1 4
Spin-offs
How and why companies spin off, and how to invest   **198**

C H A P T E R   1 5
Fad IPOs
*Accessing short-term profit opportunities while
avoiding the inevitable price plunge*   **206**

C H A P T E R   1 6
Stock Options and IPOs
Mastering the new standard in employee compensation   **214**

C O N C L U S I O N   **224**

APPENDIX A: The Underwriting Process   **232**

APPENDIX B: Analyzing the Financial Statement Items   **234**

R E S O U R C E S   **238**

N O T E S   **245**

G L O S S A R Y   **246**

I N D E X   **256**

ACKNOWLEDGMENTS

THIS BOOK WOULD not have been possible without the help of many people. I'm grateful for the tremendous help from Larrie Weil, the chief of Corporate Finance at Southwest Securities; Andrew Klein, the founder of the innovative on-line investment bank, Wit Capital; Nadine Wong, the publisher of the biotech newsletter *BioTech Navigator;* Linda Killian, the portfolio manager of the IPO Fund; Peter Schwartz, the founder of FreeEDGAR.com; Deborah Monrue, Tom Madden and Jeff Stacey from IPO Monitor.com; Drew Field, the leader in the direct IPO field; Jay Sears, vice president, marketing and business development at *EDGAR Online;* Tom Stewart-Gordon, editor of the *SCOR Report;* Steve Harmon, the Internet guru at Mecklermedia; and to my editor at Bloomberg Press, Jacqueline Murphy.

Finally, I would like to thank my business partner, Matt Harris, who had much patience while I wrote this book.

FOREWORD

N THE 1980s, the rock group Loverboy popularized the phrase, "Everybody's Working for the Weekend," in the song of the same name. In the 1990s the tune being played out from Silicon Valley to Silicon Alley is "Everybody's Working for the Equity." Translation: with bank interest rates at levels so dismal that you can measure growth in tree years, the stock market has become the virtual retirement account for millions of Americans—fully 42 percent of the U.S. adult population has a vested interest in Wall Street.

The influx of people and capital provided for a rise in the Dow, Standard and Poor's 500, Nasdaq, and most other indices. Since 1989 stocks have been on an upward spiral with more and more money pouring into mutual funds in a self-fulfilling prophecy, in which more investors fuel more gains, and so on. In the past twenty years technology stocks have come on the scene and focused attention on the initial public offering

(IPO) as a rite of passage in the well-greased capital machine that can take garage heroes like Steve Jobs or Bill Gates and thrust them into the forefront of the global economy.

The PC-based revolution in the 1980s gave rise to many well-known names in the investment sphere: Microsoft, Apple, Digital, Dell, Gateway, and Compaq, to name a few. An investor in any one of them at the IPO could have made a bundle, depending on when they sold or if they held on for the right moment to sell. In 1986 when Microsoft went public (at less than $1 a share if you factor all the splits since then) nobody cared. It was two guys from Redmond with thick glasses and polyester pants and something cryptic called MS-DOS.

Tidal waves of PC rollout, better technology, easier-to-use PC programs, and the graphical user interface invented by Xerox and popularized by Apple's

Macintosh and later Microsoft's Windows, brought technology into businesses, homes, and schools in record numbers. PCs became as common as TVs in some homes and necessary tools for any business. With that critical mass of installed users, the firms behind the tide grew in value. The stocks soared, and suddenly everyone wanted the next Intel.

Skip forward a few years. Enter the browser, the innocuous little software application that made surfing the Internet a point-and-click experience. In 1993, while the heavyweights in media and technology poured billions of dollars into digital TV dreams, a handful of pizza-eating, soda-guzzling college kids from the University of Champagne, Illinois, changed the world forever, in ways we still cannot grasp, by creating Mosaic. Mosaic was a few lines of obscure code that allowed everyday people to point and click their way around the sea of information called the Internet.

From that humble effort sprung a commercialized software product and Netscape Communications Corp., led by one of those college kids, Marc Andreessen, and Silicon Graphics founder Jim Clark, disenchanted with the interactive TV debacle and looking for the real "next big thing." They both found it in the World Wide Web.

Netscape's spectacular rise, fueled by the smart money from venture capital firm Kleiner Perkins, launched itself into the IPO record books on day one and ignited an Internet stock offering bonanza that has yet really to die down.Yes, the earlier Internet IPOs from companies such as Netcom and Mecklermedia started the interest rolling, but Netscape's tsunami woke Wall Street up to the fever and fun on IPOs at full throttle.

Given the wide-open opportunity that is the Internet, and the tremendous creativity, capital, and connectivity colliding in this space, the rekindled interest in IPOs is now at phenomenal levels. Thanks to the Internet, information about new stock offers is available to tens of millions of people who no longer have to hire a broker to get the information. They also no longer need a broker to get in on IPOs offered directly over the Internet. But the better offerings still tend to go through trusted underwriters, and the institutions often get first dibs on these, simply because only the large funds can digest the huge blocks of shares that quickly. Yet as the information flow has opened up, the demand from individual investors to "get in on" an IPO is at the highest level it's ever been. Are all IPOs winners?

Where biotechs flared and fizzled in the early 1990s, I expect Internet stocks to continue to grow. It is not a fad; look around you. The Web is everywhere—from your business card to movie billboard to TV screen. These differences translate into the fact that not all IPOs are created equal, so individual investors need to be smart about the IPO process.

As more and more people look to stocks as their future retirement, and to IPOs as being a potential instant payday, Tom Taulli's book is timely indeed. Those who don't understand IPOs are destined to get burned by them. Those who do can put their knowledge to work for their future.

— STEVE HARMON
Vice President, Business Development,
Senior Investment Analyst, Mecklermedia,
The Internet Media Company
Author of *The Internet Stock Report*
www.isdex.com

INTRODUCTION

I T WAS A SIMPLE IDEA: Offer savvy consumers the opportunity to buy and sell merchandise—such as beanie babies, artwork, baseball cards, rare coins, computers, toys—on the Internet, using an auction model. Basically, this was the creation of an on-line garage sale.

It was Pierre Omidyar who dreamed up this concept, and his business was called eBay. He was the only employee and a mere 28 years old when he started the business in 1995. And business surged. By June 1998, eBay had hosted over 15 million auctions, resulting in $340 million in sales. The company was profitable—a very rare thing in the Internet world.

Then, on September 24, 1998, eBay went public, selling 3.4 million shares to the public at $18 per share (thus raising about $62 million for the company). At the end of the day the stock closed at 47.38 per share—a stunning 163 percent increase.

But the stock did not stop there. In two months, it had soared 544 percent, making Omidyar a billionaire. In fact, eBay was not the only red-hot IPO in 1998. Here are some first-day gains of other IPOs:

◆ Broadcast.com (July): 248 percent

◆ Earthweb (November): 247 percent

◆ TicketMaster-CitySearch (December): 187 percent

◆ uBid.com (December): 166 percent

◆ GeoCities (August): 119 percent

◆ ISS Group (March): 83 percent

◆ VeriSign (January): 82 percent

Ironically, it was on a November Friday the 13th that there was the biggest IPO ever. The company was theglobe.com, an Internet site that gives away Web addresses. The offering price was $9 and within minutes the stock hit $97. By the end of trading the stock was $63, a 705 percent gain. The two founders of the company were 24 years old.

It's a fact that IPOs make one of the best places in the financial markets to find huge gainers. There's enormous upside if you can manage to pick the winners at the right time. Yes, it's a tricky and risky feat—but this book was written to bring investors closer to solving the puzzle.

You may have heard that IPOs are allocated first to wealthy individuals and institutions. It's true; those with a large capital base typically have first pick of IPOs. This is the case with any type of investment, even though the situation is changing as the Internet brings us all closer to investment opportunities. But the playing field is not equal yet—being wealthy still carries its privileges.

For example, in 1995 Michael Jordan, the star basketball player for the Chicago Bulls, was able to purchase 217,392 shares of the Oakley IPO, because he endorsed the company's sunglasses. Then there was Demi Moore, who was the recipient of about 650,000 shares of the Planet Hollywood IPO at the offering price.

However, with the emergence of the Internet, individual investors are starting to participate in IPOs.

For example, E*TRADE allowed its customers to invest in eBay and GeoCities. Wit Capital made it possible for its subscribers to buy shares of EarthWeb, TicketMaster, and uBid. Some opportunities are there for the taking. Also, you don't need to invest on the first day to make money in IPOs. For example, the institutions and wealthy individuals that purchase IPOs usually do so to generate a quick profit. This is known as *flipping*. While a one-day 50 percent or more profit is tremendous, you may be missing out on much more upside still to come. Consider those investors who flipped the Microsoft offering. Of course, they have regretted it ever since.

Successful IPO investing involves being patient. The only way to get rich overnight is through lottery or inheritance. Besides, short-term investing is a game for professionals, who have the time and resources to devote their life to investing. Playing against them is very dangerous to the survival of your portfolio.

However, being an individual investor also has many advantages in the IPO world. Since the IPO market consists mostly of small companies, much of Wall Street will probably ignore these newer companies. Wall Street likes covering the big players, such as Microsoft, Exxon, and IBM. Normally an IPO has but a few analysts covering it (and in some cases, none). This gives the individual investor an edge, since the IPO stock may not fully reflect what's happening to the company.

Another advantage to investing in IPOs is that analysis is much easier. It does not take as much work to study a small company, which may have only a few products or services, as it does to understand a multinational company, which has its hands in a variety of industries. These factors do not mean that investing in IPOs is simple or that there is a "secret formula" for finding big gains. Rather, it requires a large amount of work. But remember—it is worth it.

Of course, IPOs can be extremely risky. There are many IPOs that have collapsed—the value of some of them has been reduced to pennies. After all, small companies can be adversely affected by numerous factors including a top manager who bails out or a major customer that goes to another vendor. But this book will help you screen IPOs and decide which opportunities to take, and which to quickly and firmly pass by. Investing in IPOs can be a wild ride.

IPOs are unpredictable, but, then again, buying the "no-brainer" blue-chip stocks can be risky, too. Just look at the performances of International Harvester, United Fruit, Pennsylvania Railroad, Woolworth's, and Western Union. Let's consider another example: you could have bought U.S. Steel in 1959 for $100 per share. At that time, it was a bellwether. Everyone marveled at it as a symbol of America's strength. It was a company that, when there was a labor strike, would get the attention of the President of the United States. Despite its past prestige, by 1993 the stock was selling for under $50 per share. Even seemingly super-growth stocks can have stunning losses, such as Oracle's 30 percent one-day drop in late 1997.

As with any effective investment strategy, the way to deal with risk is to diversify. You might, for example (depending on your risk profile), invest 5 percent of your net worth in IPOs. You can then allocate the rest of your funds in other asset classes, such as blue chips, bonds, or gold.

In fact, chances are that you have already participated in the IPO market and don't realize it. How is this possible? The reason is that mutual funds are the biggest purchasers of IPOs. For example, Fidelity constitutes 10 percent of the IPO market share in the United States. So, if you own mutual funds, you likely own IPOs.

Also, you might be an employee of a company that in the future will go public. A major trend in compensation is the granting of stock options—a tremendous motivator for employees. If a company does go public, the owners of these stock options stand to make a great deal of money. So, it's important to understand the IPO game. You don't want to lose what could potentially become millions of dollars.

Despite what you might hear, you do not need a degree from the Wharton School of Business to successfully invest in IPOs (in fact, it might help if you don't have such a degree). Top-name investors, such as Warren Buffet, Peter Lynch, and Michael Price, all tout simple strategies. Leave the complicated intricacies of hedging to the pros.

This book will provide you with easy-to-understand strategies for taking advantage of the opportunities in the IPO market. The analysis involves both quantitative and qualitative factors. We will dig into financial statements. We will study risk factors. We will look at market growth of important IPO sectors such as high-tech and financial services. We will investigate the backgrounds of management. We will see how solid the underwriter is. We'll even present the best sources of IPO intelligence and market research.

And as you gain a better understanding of the IPO market, you will see that it is very exciting. You have the opportunity to investigate cutting-edge companies that are reshaping the economy. You will be glimpsing the products and services of the future.

Within a very short period, the investment world has undergone revolutionary change that gives you and me access to investments that were once only available to big financial institutions. What you make of these opportunities is entirely up to you. It's now just a matter doing your homework before you invest.

Let's get started.

INTRODUCING
IPOs

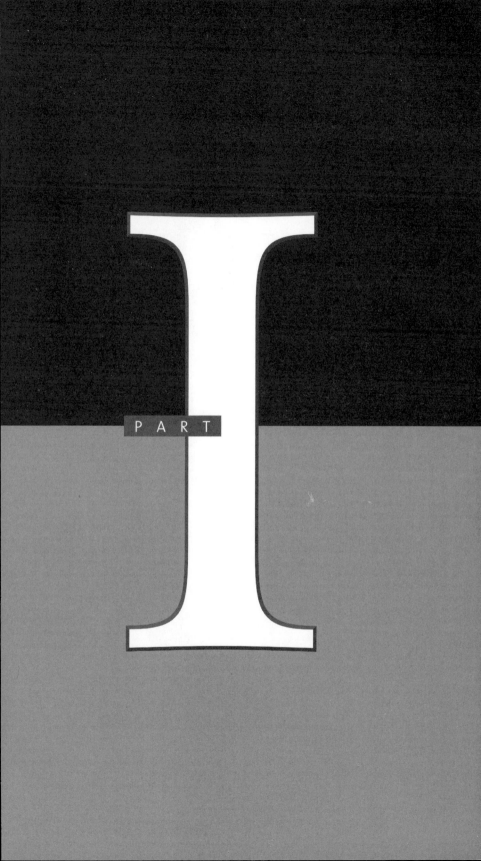

PART

I

CHAPTER

1

IPO
BASICS

T'S A COMMON misconception that IPOs are a guaranteed road to riches. Although there are many IPOs that do extremely well, the fact is that IPOs are like any other investment: there are no guarantees. Before considering IPO investment strategies, it's important for investors to understand what IPOs are and how they work.

Anyone reading this book probably knows that an initial public offering (IPO) is the first sale of stock by a company to the public. It's when a company makes the transformation from being privately held to becoming publicly traded, complete with its own ticker symbol. However, there's probably a lot of other, more advanced IPO terminology that most people don't know. For example: What does it mean when an IPO goes "effective"? What is the registration statement? What is the "red herring"? What exactly do the underwriters do? These questions—plus a great deal more about investing in IPOs—are covered in this book.

This chapter takes a look at what motivates a company to launch an initial public offering. We will also meet the major players in the IPO process.

WHY DO COMPANIES GO PUBLIC?

THERE IS NO single answer to that question. It's a major decision that will surely change the character of a company and mean many sleepless nights for management. What's more, an IPO is very expensive. The company will need to hire attorneys, accountants, printers, and many other advisers described later in this chapter.

These are the main reasons a company might decide to go public:

PRESTIGE

AN IPO IS A *major* accomplishment. Wall Street will suddenly begin to take notice. Analysts will start following the company; so will the press. And hiring new employees will become easier because publicly traded companies are generally perceived to be more stable than private companies. In fact, the company might even choose to offer employee stock options as compensation or as part of a retirement plan. Management benefits from offering stock option incentives through tax advantages and by conserving cash flow. In addition, stock incentives can cement an employee's stake in the company.

GETTING RICH

STAGING AN IPO is one of the best ways for company principals to get rich. For example, in April 1994, Christopher Klaus founded Internet Services Systems (ISS), from his grandmother's guest room. He started the company while he was a student at Georgia Institute of Technology. He developed shareware—called Internet Scanner—which allows companies to protect their computer networks. His first client, an Italian company, paid him $1,000. Then, through a referral from his lawyer, Klaus contacted Kevin O'Connor, the founder of another hot Internet company, DoubleClick. O'Connor invested $50,000 in Klaus' company, a stake that is now worth $26 million.

From there ISS grew at an astronomical rate, moving from $257,000 in sales in 1995 to $13 million in 1997, and the number of employees surged from seven to 141. When his company went public in early 1998, Klaus owned 26.1 percent of the stock. Within a week, this 24-year-old was worth a mind-boggling $160 million. Yes, enough money to pay off his school loans.

However, it's not just the founders who get rich; a company's employees can, too: Microsoft has created over 2,000 millionaires because of stock options. Another example is Apple Computer, which went public in 1980: On the first day of trading, forty employees became instant millionaires.

And, of course, need I remind the reader that anyone could have bought shares in Microsoft, ISS, and Apple on the open market? As discussed in the Introduction, if you had bought 1,000 shares of Microsoft in 1986, by November 30, 1998, you would have been worth $8,784,000.

CASH INFUSION

AN IPO WILL TYPICALLY raise a lot of cash for a company. This money does not have to be paid back. It can be used to build new facilities, fund research and development, and float the acquisition of a new or expanded business.

Some examples:

◆ In January 1998, Keebler Foods (KBL), which sells products under brands such as Cheez-It, Ready-Crust, and Carr's, issued 11.6 million shares in an IPO for $24 each, raising $278 million.

◆ In February 1998, DoubleClick (DCLK), the on-line advertising network, raised a total of $51 million. Originally, the company indicated it would sell 2.5 million shares at between $12 to $14 each. Because of intense demand, the company increased the number of shares to 3 million and sold the offering for $17 per share. On the first day of trading, the stock soared 72 percent.

All this was cash raised from initial public offerings.

LIQUIDITY

OVERALL, BECAUSE OF the large amount of capital raised from an offering, an IPO gives a company the increased ability to raise even more money. For example, banks are more willing to lend money and extend credit to publicly traded companies. And stock can be used as collateral for loans, a practice used by Lawrence Ellison, the founder of Oracle, for many of the company's early years.

An IPO also allows the founders to diversify their holdings. For example, in the ISS IPO, Klaus sold 100,000 shares of his stock and Kevin O'Connor sold 55,000 shares. This transaction was legitimate; but be wary of founders selling a large amount of stock at the time of the IPO. This is what is known as a "bail out" and may be an indication of a bad offering. After all, the founders know if the company has sound prospects for growth. In some instances the founders don't sell any of their own shares, as was the case with Yahoo! The cofounders, Jerry Yang and David Filo, did not unload any of their 4,003,750 shares.

STOCK AS CURRENCY

ANOTHER MAJOR ADVANTAGE of an IPO is that a company can use its stock as currency to purchase other businesses. Because of the lack of liquidity, and because they are hard to value, private companies often have difficulty acquiring other businesses. Suppose, for example, that a private firm wants to buy your company, but that you also have a similarly attractive offer from Microsoft. What suitor would you be more comfortable with? In most cases, your answer would be the established, recognized company.

Using stock as currency for acquisitions is a fairly common practice. In February 1998, RealNetworks acquired Vivo, one of its competitors. All shares of Vivo were exchanged for 1.1 million RealNetworks shares—for a valuation of $17.1 million.

HOWEVER, AN IPO is not the answer in every case. There are many reasons why a company should decide not to do an IPO. Here are some of them:

EXPENSE

DOING AN IPO is extremely expensive, but it's not just the monetary costs that are a factor. Having management divert huge amounts of time and effort preparing for the IPO can drain normal operations.

The biggest money pit that comes with an IPO is known as the *underwriter's discount.* This fee ranges from 5 percent to 10 percent of the amount raised in the offering. Beyond that, there are billable hours of attorney and

THE COST OF AN IPO

THIS IS AN itemized list of costs for the IPO of RealNetworks, an Internet video/audio technology company:

Securities and Exchange Commission Registration Fee	$13,591
NASD Filing Fee	$4,985
Nasdaq National Market Listing Fee	$50,000
Legal Fees and Expenses	$325,000
Accountants' Fees and Expenses	$225,000
Blue Sky Filing and Counsel Fees and Expenses	$5,000
Printing and Engraving Expenses	$150,000
Transfer Agent and Registrar Fees	$10,000
Miscellaneous Expenses	$166,424
TOTAL	$950,000

accountant fees. Printing costs (the paperwork is mind boggling) and filing fees for both the federal government and the states in which the IPO will be offered push the bill even higher.

DOING BUSINESS AS A PUBLIC COMPANY

ONCE A COMPANY goes public, the large expenses continue. For instance, publicly traded companies are required to make certain quarterly and annual filings. They need an investor's relations department to deal with shareholder inquires and will probably need to retain attorneys and accountants to handle securities and SEC compliance matters. To handle the new reporting requirements, a company will need to implement state-of-the-art accounting and information systems.

LOSS OF PRIVACY

WHEN A COMPANY initiates an IPO, it must comply with the myriad regulations meant to protect investors. A company must disclose all "material" information. For example, in the prospectus (which is the document given to

CDNOW—PRIVATE FINANCING HISTORY

THE BROTHERS JASON and Matthew Olim (both now 28 years old) were not satisfied buying CDs at the major retail stores. The markup was high, service was mediocre, and the selection focused mostly on the hits.

When the Internet started to take off, the brothers decided to sell CDs on-line. It was February 1994 when CDNow was started from their parent's home in Jenkintown, Pennsylvania.

Private financing came from the following sources:

- **Spring 1995** $81,923, Lent to them by their father.
- **December 1995** Loan from private angel Alan Meltzer, who became a company director. Meltzer had been the Chairman and CEO of Wind-Up Entertainment, a New York record label, and the founder of CD One Stop, a distributor of CDs.
- **November 1996** Short-term loans of $250,000 from Saltzman Music Partners. These loans were repaid in July 1997.
- **December 1996** Meltzer purchased $1.2 million of stock in CDNow, establishing a large equity stake in the company.
- **July 1997** the company raised venture capital money by selling Series A Convertible Preferred Stock to Keystone Ventures, a VC firm. John Regan, the Vice President of Keystone Ventures, was placed on the Board of Directors of CDNow.
- **August 1997** The VC firm Grotech infused money in exchange for Series B Convertible Preferred Stock. Patrick Kerins, the Managing Director of Grotech, was placed on the Board of Directors of CDNow.
- The VC firm ABS purchased 62,000 shares of Series B Preferred.
- Grotech received warrants to purchase up to 18,349 shares of CDNow Series B Preferred Stock.
- The investment bank of BT Alex. Brown also got warrants to purchase 103,211 shares of Series B Preferred Stock.
- **November 1997** CDNow borrowed $6.8 million from investors. According to the loan agreement, the borrowings were paid off when the company went public.

those who want to invest in an IPO), a company must disclose its financial reports, business strategies, customers, executive compensation, and risk factors. Not much is left to the imagination.

CAST OF CHARACTERS

IN ADDITION TO the company principals, many other parties take part in an IPO. Here are some of the major ones:

VENTURE CAPITALISTS

BEFORE THE IPO process can be put into motion, a company needs to attract financial support. It's several years—at least—before a start-up is ready for a public offering. The first step is for the company to seek capital from friends, family, and angels. Angels are the private investors who fund start-ups, many being entrepreneurs who have amassed fortunes by taking their own companies public, and now invest in other ventures.

The boxed example at left is a good illustration of several types of financing arrangements, made mostly by angels and venture capitalists.

For the most part, only high-net-worth individuals participate in these private transactions because they are quite complex and risky, and because they are difficult for the SEC to regulate.

For individual investors, however, it's important to note that examining early stage financing can be useful in determining an IPO's chance for success. In the December issue of *The Journal of Finance,* Alon Brav and Paul Gompers (both well-regarded finance professors) did a comprehensive study of the performance of IPOs for companies that had venture capital and those that did not. The conclusion was that companies with VC backing over the past five years returned, on average, 44.6 percent, compared to 22.5 percent for non-VC-backed firms.

According to the authors of that article, there are many reasons for these results. First of all, venture capital partners are typically put on the board of the company in which they are investing. The VC can then help provide contacts and valuable leads on additional financing. The VC can also attract analysts to follow the firm. What's more, institutions are more comfortable buying stock from companies backed by venture capitalists.

So how did CDNow perform in its IPO? The offering price was $16, and the company raised $65.6 million. The stock traded as high as $28 in April 1988. After the offering, both brothers each owned three million shares; that is, each was worth about $84 million.

However the stock later fell and sold for just $7 in September 1998. The main reason for the fall was that AMAZON.com entered the music business and within the first quarter was the biggest on-line music retailer. Thus, even though there may be a lot of smart money and strong underwriters involved in an IPO, there is no guarantee of long-term success. Investing in IPOs is definitely a high-risk game. The results vary.

AUDITOR

THE PURPOSE OF an auditor in the IPO process is to vouch for the accuracy of a company's financial statements. An analysis ensures that the company's accounting practices are consistent with generally accepted accounting procedures (GAAP). The auditor is required to be independent of the company in order to avoid any conflict of interest.

Auditors will also help the IPO candidate draft the financial reports in compliance with SEC requirements, and will issue a "comfort letter" that the underwriter uses for due diligence.

Having an experienced, well-regarded auditor is very important. If the audit is mismanaged, the IPO may be delayed by SEC questions about the financial data. Another key advantage of having strong auditors is that they can help devise an effective budget and a long-term planning process for the company. These basic tools enable the public company to forecast cash flows, plan for new capital expenditures, control interest costs, and structure a tax-efficient compensation package for managers.

ATTORNEYS

CONDUCTING AN IPO requires a team of attorneys to deal with the many complex regulations for proper state and federal compliance and disclosure. Talented legal counsel is absolutely essential to any IPO. If counsel makes mistakes, the IPO could be a disaster.

The role of the attorneys is to review existing contracts, amend the articles of incorporation and bylaws, develop stock incentive plans, readjust the capital structure, and so on. They will help deal with the officials at the SEC, review the registration documents, and provide advice on what management can and cannot say to the public.

In some cases, a company will, out of loyalty, use the attorneys they have dealt with since inception. Although this will ensure that the attorneys are very familiar with the company's practices, it may also be problematic if counsel does not have the necessary IPO experience.

FINANCIAL PRINTER

IPOS GENERATE A blizzard of paperwork. A prospectus, for example, can easily be 300 to 400 pages long. Depending on the size of the offering, a company may have to send out thousands of prospectuses across the United States and throughout the world. The printing must typically be done on very short notice—in many cases within 24 hours. What's more, there can be no typos—the document must be flawless, as the SEC requires.

There are about twenty financial printers that specialize in IPOs and are familiar with the myriad of SEC rules regarding filing format, such as paper, type size and font, colors, etc. In other words, having your neighborhood copier company do the printing would be a disaster.

Interestingly enough, when *Wired* magazine attempted

to go public in 1996, there was so much disagreement between the company and its underwriter (Goldman Sachs) regarding the font style, it should have been a warning sign that the offering was in trouble. Believe it or not, such seemingly insignificant things can wreck a deal.

PUBLIC RELATIONS FIRMS

PUBLIC RELATIONS FIRMS are crucial in stock offerings. After all, PR is a powerful tool for attracting investors. There are many companies going public these days—all competing for the attention of the press and investors. Without good PR, an IPO can easily be lost in the crowd.

However, as with most things financial, the SEC has certain guidelines regarding public relations. The company cannot disclose anything that varies from the contents of the prospectus. If this rule is violated, the company could suffer serious consequences—such as the SEC terminating the offering. PR firms that specialize in IPO marketing know the rules and know how to get the message out to the right brokers, investors, institutions, analysts, and market makers.

Unfortunately, some companies use PR to cloud the facts. This type of misleading information is sometimes found in obscure offerings from unknown companies. Therefore, it is wise for investors to be skeptical of information contained in the press releases. After all, some of the facts are bound to be glossed over in the spin. It's better to focus on the facts contained in the prospectus.

TRANSFER AGENT/REGISTRAR

THE ROLE OF the transfer agent is to maintain shareholder information. For example, the transfer agent will hold the name, address, Social Security number, and number of shares purchased for each shareholder. In an IPO it is the transfer agent who handles the physical delivery of stock certificates to those who have indicated interest in purchasing shares. When the stock begins trading, the transfer agent will handle the transfer of stock certificates in every buy-sell transaction.

The registrar, on the other hand, ensures that the correct number of shares are exchanged when there is a buy-sell transaction. The registrar will also keep records of destroyed, canceled, or lost stock certificates.

The company doing the IPO will typically hire an outside firm, such as a bank, to act as the transfer agent. In most cases, this firm will act as both the transfer agent and the registrar.

UNDERWRITERS

UNDERWRITERS PLAY A pivotal role in executing a successful initial public offering. The managing underwriters are the investment bankers who run the IPO show. They deter-

SYNDICATE COMPANIES FOR CDNOW

SYNDICATED COMPANIES	SHARES
BT Alex. Brown Incorporated	1,700,000
NationsBanc Montgomery Securities LLC	1,200,000
Donaldson, Lufkin & Jenrette Securities Corporation	100,000
Furman Selz LLC	100,000
Hambrecht & Quist LLC	100,000
Morgan Stanley & Co. Incorporated	100,000
Boenning & Scattergood Incorporated	80,000
Dominick & Dominick, Incorporated	80,000
Fahnestock & Co. Incorporated	80,000
Genesis Merchant Group Securities	80,000
Janney Montgomery Scott Incorporated	80,000
The Ohio Company	80,000
Parker/Hunter Incorporated	80,000
Pennsylvania Merchant Group LTD	80,000
Sanders Morris Mundy Incorporated	80,000
Wessels, Arnold & Henderson, LLC	80,000
TOTAL	4,100,000

NOTE: BT Alex. Brown and NationsBanc Montgomery Securities were the lead underwriters.

mine the price of the offering; help draft the prospectus and other filing documents; conduct due diligence; and most importantly, find investors for the offering. In many cases, the underwriter will continue to provide services even after the IPO is completed. For example, the underwriter might advise the newly public company on matters such as mergers and acquisitions or debt offerings.

The managing underwriters will also assemble a group of syndicate underwriters. It is the syndicate that helps sell the IPO's stock to the public. The main reason for a syndicate is to share liability—that is, if there is a shareholder's lawsuit, the liability can be dispersed.

It's hard to exaggerate the importance of an underwriter. Having the right one in place can mean the difference between a successful IPO and a failed offering. So, before you invest in any IPO, it makes sense to investigate the underwriter. Interestingly enough, the underwriting business is the prime source of revenue for securities firms. For more information on types of underwriters, see Appendix A on page 232.

This chapter is meant as a general overview to give the reader a sense of the IPO world. The next section goes into greater detail on the IPO process. It is surprising that even many investment professionals do not understand some of the changing intricacies of IPOs. However, to be a successful IPO investor, it is imperative to know how the procedure works.

CHAPTER

The IPO
PROCESS

T HIS CHAPTER TAKES a look at the IPO process from the moment when management decides to do an IPO to the time when shares are sold to the public. These are the basic steps that precede an initial public offering:

◆ Due diligence is conducted

◆ Letter of Intent is signed

◆ Registration Statement is drafted and filed with the Securities and Exchange Commission

◆ The road show begins the marketing

◆ Investors are solicited

◆ The company chooses a listed exchange or OTC market

◆ The offering is finalized

The IPO process is more complicated than many investors realize. Before examining each step, take a quick look at the descriptions of the legislation that governs IPOs.

LAWS THAT LEGISLATE IPOS

TWO PRIMARY FEDERAL statutes that cover IPOs were legislated during the Great Depression after abuses in the stock market during the 1920s. The Securities and Exchange Commission (SEC) enforces these laws:

◆ **Securities Act of 1933.** This "Truth in Securities" Act requires that before any stock is sold to the general public, the securities must be registered with the SEC. The prospectus can contain no material misstatements. Such misstatements can lead the SEC to file civil and criminal sanctions against the company and its underwriters.

◆ **Securities Exchange Act of 1934.** This requires that a registered public company make periodic disclosures. Furthermore, the Act has sanctions for violations of unfair market practices, such as insider trading.

In addition to these federal laws, there are also state

laws called "blue sky laws" regulating IPOs. The name is derived from a nineteenth-century court case in which the judge compared a stock offering to someone selling the blue sky. These laws are important because they dictate the logistics of the IPO process.

DUE DILIGENCE

BEFORE AN IPO can get rolling, underwriters must perform due diligence on the company—an extensive investigation. They visit offices, conduct interviews, analyze the financial statements, scrutinize the accounting procedures, and consult with the auditors. The best underwriters will even talk to customers and suppliers. The purpose of a due diligence investigation is to minimize the legal risk to underwriters, because they are liable for material misstatements in the prospectus, just as the company itself is liable.

If, after due diligence, the underwriters are satisfied with the company's prospects, and are interested in orchestrating the offering, a letter of intent will be drafted and signed.

LETTER OF INTENT

A LETTER OF INTENT is an understanding between the company and the underwriter. It sets forth the tentative terms of the relationship, like the percentage of ownership, minimum/maximum amount of money to be raised, counsel for the underwriter, counsel for the company, compensation for the underwriter, etc. The letter of intent also establishes a range for the offering price of the issue. For example, the price range may be $14 to $18, but over time this price may be adjusted. Since it may take several months to get approval for the offering, it is virtually impossible to determine an exact price for the stock.

A letter of intent is little more than an agreement to agree. It is not a binding contract. A final agreement is not usually signed until the day before, or on the morning of, the offering. The company's responsibility to pay all the fees for professional services, however, is binding after the letter of intent is signed. Though cancellations are rare, the collapse of an IPO can leave the company with debilitating expenses.

The final underwriting agreement is identical to the letter of intent except for the addition of the final stock price and number of shares to be issued. There will also need to be an agreement among underwriters. This document expresses the number of shares to be allocated among the comanagers and syndicate underwriters and enumerates the compensation breakdown.

Deciding the price of the issue is one of the most complex tasks of an underwriter. The firm will look at factors such as the valuations of prior IPOs in the same sector, and the company's stature within its industry. If a company has a proprietary technology or tremendous market share, there may be a premium to the valuation. But, ultimately, the pricing tends to be more of an art than a science.

The stock must not be priced too high, which would deter investors. In fact, offerings are typically underpriced to encourage investor participation. When the stock is offered, the price will often make a big jump on the first day. It's not uncommon to see the stock price soar 30 to 40 percent almost immediately.

VeriSign, a company that develops digital IDs for the Internet, did its IPO on January 30, 1998, with the help of the underwriters of Morgan Stanley, Dean Witter, Discover. Because of huge demand, the price was boosted from $12 to $14 per share. About 3 million shares were offered to the public (about 15 percent of the company), and at the opening, the stock increased to $17. By the end of the day, the stock was up to $25.50, an 82 percent increase. An IPO that sells at a high premium on its first day is called a "hot" IPO.

At one time it was considered an embarrassment to have such a major price increase on the first day, because it meant that the company could have raised much more money, but it's now becoming standard practice to witness these huge premiums.

In some cases there are selfish reasons for underpricing. Planning for a huge premium, for example, makes it easier for underwriters to engage in the questionable practice of *spinning*. Spinning is a routine by which an underwriter allocates a certain amount of IPO stock to potential clients (usually companies that are headed for IPOs themselves). By spinning lucrative IPOs to potential clients, underwriters are hoping to get the company's business in the future. Spinning, though, has come under heavy criticism and is currently being investigated by the SEC.

For the most part, it is very risky to purchase an IPO on the first day of its offering. There tends to be a frenzy of trading activity and price fluctuation; rationality can go out the window as investors bid on a limited number of shares. It's often safer for individual investors to wait several months and let the dust settle before buying their shares.

DRAFTING THE
REGISTRATION STATEMENT

AFTER THE LETTER of intent has been signed, the registration statement must be drafted and filed. There are two parts to the registration statement: (a) The prospectus and (b) additional information, which includes summaries of the expenses, insurance for officers and directors, the underwriting agreement, etc.

Drafting the registration is a time-consuming task. The first step in the process is called the "all-hands" meeting in which all the participants (management, attorneys, underwriters, auditors, etc.) gather to initiate the steps for creating the registration statement and are assigned their specific tasks.

The most important document in a registration statement is the prospectus, because it is the tool that is used to sell the offering to investors. Chapter 4 contains detailed information on reading and understanding an IPO prospectus.

THE TWO TYPES OF REGISTRATION STATEMENTS

◆ **Form S-1.** Any company can use an S-1, but because of its complexity, it is typically used by IPOs raising millions of dollars. The company must disclose three years' balance sheets, statements of income, shareholders' equity, and changes in financial condition. It must also give a detailed description of the business, management compensation, and facilities. Since S-1 filings tend to indicate solid companies, they have more prestige in the industry than SB filings.

◆ **Form SB.** There are two types of SB offerings. **FORM SB-1** limits the amount to be raised to $10 million, whereas **FORM SB-2** has no limit. An IPO using an SB-1 provides balance sheets for only the past fiscal year; SB-2s require two years'. SB-1s report two years' statements of income, changes in financial condition, and shareholders' equity; SB-2s disclose data from the past three years.

FILING THE REGISTRATION STATEMENT

WHEN THE REGISTRATION statement is drafted, the company may arrange a prefiling conference with the SEC to allow the company to discuss the details of the offering with regulators. This step can save much time and money, since the SEC officials will provide guidelines on what information the company should disclose.

Next, the company will file the registration statement with the SEC. At the same time, filings will be made with all the states in which the stock will be offered, as well as with the National Association of Securities Dealers (NASD). The NASD analyzes the registration statement to see if the compensation is, in their estimation, fair and equitable.

Its approval of the registration statement can take from six weeks to several months, depending on the workload of the SEC and the complexity of the deal. Before approving the filing, however, the SEC will usually have questions about the offering that are communicated through what are called "comment letters."

THE ROAD SHOW

ALSO KNOWN AS the "dog-and-pony show," the road show allows a company to generate interest from brokerage firms and institutions for the IPO. For approximately two to three weeks, the senior managers will visit financial centers, such as San Francisco, New York, and Los Angeles, to give presentations. During the typical breakfast and a slideshow, the audience can ask the managers questions.

The general public is not allowed to attend road shows. But Wit Capital, which is an on-line investment bank, is using Web video technology to give the individual investors the opportunity to view these events.

SECURING INVESTORS

BEFORE THE SEC gives its approval, it is not uncommon for the preliminary prospectus to be distributed to potential investors to generate interest. At this stage, the preliminary prospectus is known as a *red herring.* Some companies choose to wait until after the first round of comment letters before releasing the red herring to investors, in order to reduce the chance of embarrassment of having to make significant changes to the prospectus.

Regardless of when it's distributed, a red herring always contains the following disclaimer in red ink on the front of the document:

> Information contained herein is subject to completion or amendment. A registration statement relating to these securities has been filed with the SEC. These securities may not be sold nor may offers to buy be accepted prior to the time the registration statement becomes effective. This prospectus shall not constitute an offer to sell or the solicitation of an offer to buy nor shall there be any sale of these securities in any State in which such an offer, solicitation or sale would be

unlawful prior to registration or qualification under the securities laws of any such State.

Yes, this is lawyer mumbo-jumbo. However, it is important for investors to note the disclaimer and realize that the information in the prospectus is not yet final and the offering not yet approved.

Members of the underwriting syndicate use the red herring to begin locating investors for the offering. However, before a broker can even talk to a client about an IPO, he must provide the red herring for review. It is the only information that can be provided. If the investor is interested, he or she will sign an indication of interest. This does not constitute a sale, because the price has not yet been established. It is not until the day of the offering that the sale becomes final. Any broker asking for money before the day of the offering is in violation of securities laws.

During the pre-approval time, the company is in its "quiet period." As discussed above, the information released to the public must be in accordance with what is in the prospectus. The only other thing that can be published is a *tombstone ad,* as shown below. You will see these

$100,000,000

South Jersey
Gas Company

Medium-Term Note Program

Dealer

First Union Capital Markets

ads in the back of the Marketplace section of *The Wall Street Journal.* A tombstone may contain the company logo, address, the stock price, and the number of shares to be issued. According to SEC rules, the quiet period ends twenty-five days after the stock starts trading.

CHOOSING LISTED EXCHANGES OR OVER-THE-COUNTER MARKETS

BEFORE A COMPANY can issue shares to the public, it must decide in which market the shares will be listed and traded. In most cases, an IPO will be listed on the Over-the-Counter (OTC) market, which is simply a network of computers. Because many companies are relatively small when they are first public, OTC distribution makes more sense than exchange trading because exchanges have size and volume requirements that most smaller companies can't meet.

The most prestigious listed exchange is the New York Stock Exchange (NYSE). Trading on the NYSE gives a company instant visibility that translates into increased trading volume. The NYSE has a physical trading floor, where brokers buy and sell stock, and 1,300 members. To be listed on the NYSE, a company must meet minimum requirements that include having pretax earnings of $2.5 million, $18 million in assets, 1 million shares outstanding, and 2,000 shareholders.

There are some IPOs that are large enough to be listed on the NYSE. Hertz, for example, did its IPO on the NYSE in April 1997.

There are also four regional stock exchanges, all with physical trading floors: Pacific, Midwest, Philadelphia, and Boston. The companies that do IPOs on these regional exchanges tend to be small and local. Their trading is usually very light.

The over-the-counter market is more of a virtual exchange. The over-the-counter forums include:

◆ **Nasdaq NM** (National Association of Securities Dealers Automated Quotations National Market). This is the OTC market for top-tier firms. They must have a minimum of

$4 million in net assets, $750,000 in net earnings, and 400 shareholders.

Interestingly enough, even major companies are opting to list on Nasdaq instead of listed exchanges like the NYSE. Nasdaq has gained the reputation as the exchange for high tech, high-growth companies. The NYSE has a reputation for more traditional businesses—such as banking, insurance, and manufacturing. In fact, even though such companies as Microsoft, Intel, Cisco, Dell, and Oracle can easily list on the NYSE, they prefer to stay on the more hip Nasdaq.

◆ **Nasdaq Small Cap.** This exchange is for companies that cannot meet the requirements for NASDAQ NM. Qualifying factors include 300 shareholders and net assets of $2 million; no net earnings are required. Nasdaq's membership consists of 5,400 companies.

◆ **Pink Sheets.** Penny stocks are traded on the Pink Sheets. (Penny stocks are small, illiquid stocks with very little revenue. They are too risky for most individual investors.) The name is derived from the pink paper on which the quotations for this market are printed. There are about 15,000 companies listed on Pink Sheets—however, listing requirements are less rigid than NASDAQ.

◆ **Bulletin Board.** Bulletin Board provides up-to-date information—i.e., real-time quotes—on Pink Sheets stocks. This is an automated, centralized system on which approximately 6,000 stocks are listed. However, the Bulletin Board and the Pink Sheets markets are not stock exchanges. They are quotation services. What's more, both the Bulletin Board and Pink Sheets are loosely regulated. Thus, they can be dangerous for individual investors. Interestingly, some companies try to disguise the fact that they are listed on the Bulletin Board by telling investors they are listed on "Nasdaq Bulletin Board." Don't be fooled.

FINALIZATION OF THE OFFERING

AN IPO IS ready for prime time when the SEC approval is final, the underwriting agreement is signed, and the price and number of shares are set.

The "effective date" is when SEC approval is granted. After the effective date, the company is allowed to sell its shares to the public. The number of shares and price of the issue are determined on the day of the offering. This final step can be a particularly grueling process for everyone involved.

"I have seen fights over twenty-five cents between the company and the underwriter," says Larrie Weill, head of the IPO department at Southwest Securities. "Then again, a price difference of twenty-five cents can amount to $10 million."[1]

Depending on market conditions, the offering price may be set higher or lower than the estimated price range. The printer will then print a final version of the prospectus, which will be sent to all the buyers of the offering.

Once this process is complete, the company is officially public.

IPOs FOR
Investors

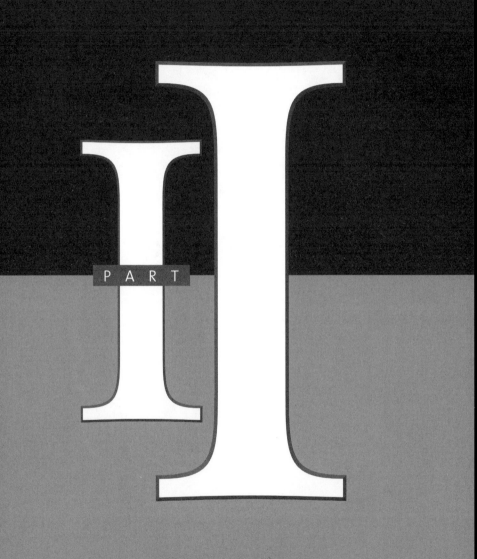

PART

I

CHAPTER

Finding The
BEST IPO
INFORMATION

THE FIRST STEP in any smart investment decision is research. But the reality is that many individuals don't spend nearly enough time investigating the soundness of their potential investments. Instead, they act on rumors, or rely on tips from their hair stylist or other questionable "experts." Sure, it is possible to get lucky with this type of advice, the stock might soar—but relying on luck is risky.

So, the first lesson for any investor is: Don't buy any IPO strictly on rumors. After all, if you're going to spend $1,000 or $5,000 or even more on a stock, isn't it a good idea to investigate the company?

At the other end of the spectrum there are investors engaging in "analysis paralysis." They think that in order to win on Wall Street you need to have the most complex, state-of-the-art investment strategies. You need to use esoteric investment vehicles, such as derivatives, and calculate extensive mathematical formulas. Thankfully, you can make a lot of money without engaging in these mental gymnastics. It has been shown time after time that good investing has everything to do with common sense—as long as it is based on a foundation of sound facts.

As recently as a few years ago it was difficult to get reliable research on companies. You had to purchase expensive subscription services—which were sent to you in the mail and arrived somewhat dated. But all that's changed. Today, the Internet and even some print publications have more than enough timely information to help you make sound investment decisions, and much of that information is free!

This chapter is designed to help you find the information you need about upcoming IPOs, to see what the analysts are saying about their chances, and to track their performance. Pay attention when you get to the EDGAR section, where you'll learn how to access information on any IPO—directly from the SEC. There is also a Resources section at the end of this book. It contains a more exhaustive listing of IPO information sources of every stripe, as well as addresses, telephone numbers, and Web sites for the sources described in this chapter.

INFORMATION TO GET
YOUR FEET WET

THERE ARE A lot of great places to read about the comings and goings of IPOs. These publications and Web sites will help you to learn the industry and to feel comfortable with the terminology. We'll describe more advanced IPO investment tools later in this chapter. But, first, let's start with some lighter-weight sources of investor information.

THE WALL STREET JOURNAL

THIS IS THE DAILY BIBLE for IPO investors—and just about every other type of investor, too. There are routinely a variety of articles on specific IPOs, plus stories on current trends in the IPO market. The "Heard on the Street" column will occasionally cover hot IPOs, and you will see frequent IPO stories from Dow Jones staff writer Dunstan Prial.

The print version of *The Wall Street Journal* costs $175 per year; the on-line edition is $49 per year ($29 if you are a subscriber to the printed version). The Web site has the same information as the printed version. In fact, in many cases, the on-line articles are longer and more up-to-date.

You can also set up your own "Personal Journal." This tool allows you to create a customized section of the *Journal* that will search for articles based on key words and phrases, such as "IPO." It's a very simple, yet powerful, tool to track IPOs. There is also a portfolio feature, with which you can track stocks. One strategy is to create a hypothetical portfolio of IPOs, and track their performance over time. It's a great way to learn about IPOs without actually risking your assets.

Any investor who is interested in investing in IPOs should get accustomed to reading *The Wall Street Journal* and using the tools offered on its Web site (www.WSJ. com).

BARRON'S

THIS IS A WEEKLY business and finance newspaper that contains in-depth analysis of companies and stocks. Their writers are not afraid to tell it like it is. And, they arguably have the best inside IPO coverage of any publication available off the newsstand. Every week there is an "IPO spotlight", written by *Barron's* staff writer Scott Reeves. Keep an eye on that feature for current IPO analysis.

All the content from the printed version is also contained in their on-line edition. If you want to subscribe, sign up for the on-line edition of *The Wall Street Journal*, and you'll have access to *Barron's* and also *Smart Money* Interactive as part of that package.

A one-year subscription to the print edition of *Barron's* is $145 (www.Barrons.com).

INTERNET STOCK REPORT

STEVE HARMON, senior investment analyst for Mecklermedia, perhaps the most-followed Internet investment analyst, writes a daily column called "The Internet Stock Report." He frequently covers the latest high-profile IPOs. His reports provide reliable quantitative and qualitative analysis–so much so that Bill Gates, John Doerr, Yahoo!'s Jerry Yang, and PC-media guru Esther Dyson are among his 250,000 followers. It's worth checking out if you're an IPO watcher and, yes, the information is free (www.InternetNews.com/stocks).

THESTREET.COM

THESTREET.COM IS THE creation of the outspoken James J. Cramer, who writes a high-profile investment column for several magazines and also runs a hedge fund. TheStreet. com is very informative and timely, and articles are posted throughout the day. If anything, it is fun to read. You will find analyses of IPOs in the "Companies" section—always strong and engaging. A subscription is $9.95 per month (www.TheStreet.Com).

MOTLEY FOOL

THE MOTLEY FOOL is a lot like TheStreet.com. Both are exclusively on-line, well-written and researched, and much fun to read. However, Motley Fool is completely free. You will see a variety of coverage on companies that are going public (www.Fool.com).

RED HERRING

THE RED HERRING is both a magazine and an on-line publication. It covers the high-tech sector. It's a great resource for information about the hottest IPOs, and for interviews with the "movers and shakers." Plus, there's great industry analysis. A one-year subscription for the print edition is $49 (www.Herring.com).

OTHER ON-LINE RESOURCES

YAHOO!, EXCITE, STOCKSITE, and Silicon Investor are other all useful Web sites to check out on a regular basis when you are researching IPOs. Yahoo! has a section called "US IPOs" which has an extensive list of the latest IPO stories. Excite has a feature called "Eye on IPOs." There is also an IPO calendar and performance information. However, to access the IPO information on Excite, you must subscribe to the S&P Personal Wealth Service, which is $9.95 per month. StockSite is geared for the active investor. Every week I write a column, "Tech Corner," on the high-tech IPO sector. You will also find a weekly column by Christopher Byron, called "Inside Scoop," which covers the smaller offerings—and he is not afraid to pull punches. I also write a daily IPO column for Silicon Investor (www.Yahoo.com; www.Excite.com; www.StockSite.com; www.SiliconInvestor.com).

IN-DEPTH IPO INFORMATION

THE INFORMATION AGE has put an end to good information on IPOs being either unavailable or proprietary. Here are some of the best places to do in-depth research on specific companies and upcoming IPOs. If you're serious about investing in IPOs, you should familiarize yourself with one or several of these resources. As you'll see, most of these databases and news services are on-line, which allows constant updating and real-time information.

BLOOMBERG

BLOOMBERG FINANCIAL MARKETS has added an IPO center to its comprehensive financial Web site. It covers all of the following, with more to come:

◆ The latest IPO listings

◆ IPO headlines from Bloomberg News

◆ The Bloomberg IPO Index, which is a capitalization-weighted index that tracks the performance of IPOs during their first year of trading (www.bloomberg.com).

IPO CENTRAL

A JOINT VENTURE between Hoover's and *EDGAR Online*, this is one of the best IPO sites on the Web. Hoover's, based in Austin, collects research on more than 12,000 U.S. and foreign companies. Even private companies are covered. *EDGAR Online* is discussed later in this chapter.

IPOCentral contains an incredible amount of useful information that is updated daily:

◆ **Latest Filings.** A list of the companies that have filed S-1s or SB-2s during the past week.

◆ **IPOs in Registration.** A complete listing of those companies that have filed a registration statement, but have yet to start trading (it takes about four to six weeks until the shares are offered).

◆ **This Week's Scheduled Pricing.** A list of companies expected to start trading in the next week.

◆ **Aftermarket Performance.** A review of how well indi-

vidual IPOs have done after trading has started.

◆ **Withdrawals and Postponements.** A listing of companies that have delayed or completely withdrawn the offering.

◆ **Find an IPO.** A search feature for an IPO based on name, keyword, underwriter, state, or metro area.

◆ **IPO Directory.** A comprehensive list of companies that have filed for an IPO on or after May 6, 1996, searchable by date or company name.

◆ **IPO Close-Up.** A weekly commentary on a current IPO.

◆ **Featured IPO.** A Hoover's Company Profile feature that must be purchased. However, every week there will be an additional featured IPO which will have a free link to a Hoover's Profile.

◆ **Beginner's Guide.** A great resource of articles and Web sites about the IPO world.

◆ **Front-Page Links.** Six to seven weekly links to IPO articles on the front page of IPOCentral.com.

Yes, everything above is free. However, if you want even more detailed information such as real-time SEC documents, financial reports, market data, and industry comparisons, then you can subscribe for $12.95 per month or $124.95 per year (www.ipoCentral.com).

IPO MONITOR

IPO MONITOR PROVIDES a comprehensive set of services for IPO information. One of its best features is its e-mail notifications, which alert subscribers to the following:

◆ **New Filings.** Daily e-mail regarding those companies that have filed a registration statement.

◆ **Going Public.** An e-mail list sent every Monday of those companies that are expected to price for the current week.

◆ **New Pricing.** An e-mail that shows which companies have been priced and are being actively traded. It is normally sent in the morning, giving you a head start to buy the IPO in the aftermarket.

◆ **Aftermarket Performance.** A weekly list of companies indicating how they have performed since their offerings.

Although you can obtain the same information by going to IPO Monitor's Web site, the e-mail notification is extremely useful. What's more, IPOMonitor has an extensive data research sheet on the Web site for any company that registers to go public. You can search for companies based on name, industry, and underwriter. The data sheet includes such things as contact information, industry classification, underwriters, description of the business, number of shares offered, expected price range, names of senior managers, major shareholders, balance sheets, and income statements.

This all-inclusive information comes with a price tag. The subscription fee is $29 per month or $290 per year (www.ipoMonitor.com).

IPO DATA SYSTEMS

IPO DATA SYSTEMS has a comprehensive database of IPO financial filings, which extend back to January 1993. There are over 2,500 detailed company profiles (the 1997 profiles are free). These profiles have over 200 items—including balance sheet, income statement, use of proceeds,

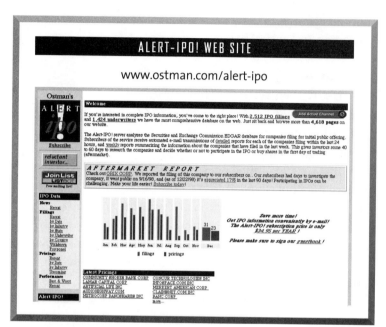

principal shareholders, and contact information.

For a subscription fee of $15 per month or $180 per year, you get the following:

◆ IPO filings for the current week
◆ Every IPO pricing for the week
◆ List of the upcoming IPOs
◆ Search of the database based on a variety of criteria (such as keywords, industry, etc.)
◆ List of IPO performance year-to-date
◆ List of the top underwriters based on number of deals, total dollar amount of the offerings, and percentage gains

There are also free sections on the site. You can read commentaries from various IPO analysts, or peruse a list of Direct Public Offerings (companies that are doing their own offerings without the assistance of an underwriter) (www.ipoData.com).

ALERT-IPO

ALERT-IPO IS ONE of the cheapest IPO subscription services. For $34.95 per year you receive weekly summaries via e-mail that detail which companies have filed for IPOs during the past week. Every day you will receive reports on each company that has filed within the past 24 to 48 hours. There are also some free areas on the site. For example, you can click to a section that provides a weekly summary report of recent filings (www.ostman.com/alert-ipo).

CBS MARKETWATCH-DBCC

THIS IS A LEADING provider of real-time financial information and commentary. Darren Chervitz is the reporter who contributes most of the IPO information including:

◆ **IPO Daily Report.** Brief descriptions of the latest companies going public.

◆ **IPO Commentary.** In-depth reports on specific IPOs. Chervitz rates each company on a scale of 1 to 5.

◆ **IPO First Words.** Interviews with investment bankers, executives, and analysts who are involved in the IPO market.

◆ **Week's IPOs.** A list of companies going public for the current week.

◆ **Pick of the Week.** An IPO investment that looks good according to the analysts at Renaissance Capital.

◆ **The ABCs of IPOs.** This is a four-part article that describes the IPO process. The site is a tremendous resource, and it is free (www.cbs.marketwatch.com).

IPO SPOTLIGHT

THE IPO SPOTLIGHT is a subscription service that can be either e-mailed to you for $30 per month or faxed for $40 per month. The service provides basic IPO information, such as the expected date of issuance, size of the deal, lead underwriters, and so on.

What makes the service unique is that it provides recommendations on which IPOs to buy. But, be wary of some of the claims it makes: "get in on the IPOs with the great profit potential, without the research and prospectus study normally required." This is probably not a good idea—you want to make sure you understand exactly what you are investing in (www.ipoSpotlight.com).

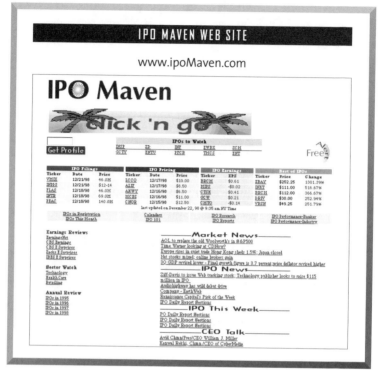

IPO MAVEN

MANISH SHAH, A widely quoted authority of the IPO market, manages the IPO Maven site. It provides the following:

◆ **CEO Talk.** Interviews with the CEOs of public companies.

◆ **Stock Watch.** A list of IPOs that look promising.

◆ **Market Summary.** Several paragraphs describing each of the latest IPOs.

◆ **Company Stories.** In-depth analyses of various companies (although, not all of them are IPOs).

◆ **Q & A.** Articles that describe the ABCs of IPOs.

◆ **Calendars.** A list of upcoming IPOs, as well as those companies that have postponed or withdrawn their offerings.

◆ **IPO Performance.** An overview of sectors, showing which are the hottest and which are the worst.

◆ **IPO Research.** A snapshot look at various IPOs.

◆ **IPO Alert.** E-mail notifications of companies that registered to initiate an IPO, pricings, and top stock gainers/losers (www.ipoMaven.com).

EDGAR RESOURCES

SEC'S EDGAR

THE FIRST PLACE I VISIT to investigate any IPO is EDGAR, which stands for Electronic Data Gathering Analysis and Retrieval. This huge on-line database of financial filings was developed by the SEC.

Any company that files a registration for an S-1, SB-1, or SB-2 offering must present an electronic version of the filing, which is placed in the EDGAR database. In other words, by going to the EDGAR site, you can get the full version of any company's prospectus. And, as we will see in the next chapter, it is in the prospectus that you will find much of the necessary information to help make investment decisions. But you cannot retrieve EDGAR filings in real time. Rather, there is a twenty-four- to forty-eight-hour delay.

EDGAR is not very pretty graphically. The filings you download are in raw form and you will often see spaces in the lines of text. But, then again, the information is free. And you get everything you need to examine an initial public offering.

You can search the database in following ways:

◆ **Natural language.** As the words imply, you can enter a full-sentence search statement, such as "Show me all the filings for Microsoft."

◆ **Boolean operators.** You use such keywords as "and," "not," and "adj." So, if you want to find documents that have both filings for Microsoft and Intel, you specify, "Show me the documents for Microsoft *and* Intel." If you want documents from either Microsoft or Intel, then use "or." If you want to exclude something from the search, then use "not." For example: "Search all documents for Microsoft *not* Intel." As for "adj," this stands for adjacent and means that two words must always be together. So, if you specify the search of "cordless *adj* telephone," then you will get those documents that only have "cordless telephone."

◆ **Wildcards.** The asterisk character ("*") indicates to the search engine to match the words that precede the * and to ignore any trailing characters. For example, if you specify "Micro*", you will get matches for Microsoft, Microsystems, and so on (www.sec.gov).

THERE ARE SOME other useful sites and tools that use EDGAR's information in a more aesthetically-pleasing format. These include:

FreeEDGAR

THIS SITE HAS TWO software products that are worth exploring:

1 Excel Add-In. This software allows Excel 97 to download prospectuses and other financial statements. Since you are not using your browser, the download process is fast. The add-in has its own predefined spreadsheets to analyze the financial information, or, you can create your own spreadsheets. This is a very powerful tool that's easy to use. By using just a few clicks, you're done.

2 Watchlist. You can create a custom list of companies that you're interested in tracking, and FreeEDGAR will notify you via e-mail whenever there is information. So far, FreeEDGAR is the only company offering free, unlimited access to real-time corporate data filed with the Securities and Exchange Commission (it costs the company about $300,000 per year for the data feed) (www.FreeEdgar.com).

EDGAR ONLINE

LIKE FreeEDGAR, *EdgarOnline* provides real-time access to financial filings from the SEC. There is a subscription cost, but also many benefits:

◆ You can download the filings into MSWord or other programs that support RTF (Rich Text Format).

◆ Real-time notification of filings via e-mail, based on a watch list.

◆ Use of toll-free customer support and e-mail support (in fact, you get this free even if you are not a subscriber).

◆ Extensive searching capabilities of the database (company name, ticker symbol, form type, sector, industries, geographic location, and date range).

◆ Access to other valued-added financial content, such as PC Quote, BigCharts, Hoover's, and Zack's.

◆ A database extending back to 1994.

◆ *EDGAR Online* People is a great resource that allows the user to search financial statements to obtain background information, such as compensation, on officers and significant owners of public companies. No other site has this type of research capability.

The subscriptions start at $9.95 per month; the fee is based on how many filings you download. As for the free services, you get all the benefits listed above, except the data is not real time. However, for most investors, you do not need real-time data. Even if the data is delayed several days, it should not make a difference because it takes four to six weeks for the IPO to occur (www.edgar-online.com).

OTHER IPO INFORMATION RESOURCES

NEWSLETTERS

THERE ARE THOUSANDS of investment newsletters, many costing upwards of $500 per year. But the choices are less confusing for the IPO investor, since there are only a few newsletters that cover this sector:

◆ **New Issues.** The editor, Norman Fosback, has a vast understanding of the IPO market. There are articles about the general conditions of the IPO market, as well as profiles on individual companies. When you subscribe, you get a free book, written by Fosback, called *Stock Market Logic.* The newsletter is issued every month and also has e-mail alerts; $95 per year (800-442-9000).

◆ **The IPO Reporter.** Each issue has several pages of commentary on the latest trends in the IPO market, as well as stock recommendations. This newsletter is published on the first and fifteenth of every month, and the annual subscription rate is $270 (212- 765-5311).

◆ **Going Public.** This newsletter is very similar to *The IPO Insider* and *New Issues.* There is general commentary and individual company profiles, as well as IPO calendars. The newsletter has 50 issues per year for $1,245 (212-432-0045).

CHAT ROOMS/DISCUSSION GROUP

THESE CAN BE VERY worthwhile for investors who want expert answers to questions. But you should also be skeptical of what you read on message boards—there is no real way of knowing who is posting a message. True, it could be from someone who understands the investment. But the respondent may also be a former investor who has an axe to grind, or the CEO who wants to pump up the stock.

Disregard messages like "This stock will go up 600 percent in two months" or "This stock will definitely go bust."

In fact, a variety of phony IPOs have been orchestrated by using discussion groups. Be skeptical of information that seems too good to be true. Check out the discussion boards listed in this book's Resources section.

COMPANY WEB SITES

IF YOU WANT information on a specific company, why not go right to the source? Looking at the Web site of the company doing the IPO can be a tremendous resource. You will see press releases, bios on the management, a customer/partner list, testimonials, case studies, and a lot of other detailed content. But, as you might suspect, this isn't the place to look for unbiased, hard-hitting data. Expect to find mostly public relations-approved news.

YOUR BROKER

A FINAL SOURCE OF information on IPOs is your stock broker. Many brokerage firms have access to research that is not accessible to the general public. And, if you're lucky, your broker may have heard the buzz on the Street regarding an upcoming IPO and be willing to share information with you.

INFORMATION TO STAY AWAY FROM

NOT ALL INFORMATION is good information. Here are some IPO information sources to avoid:

◆ **Spam.** Spam is unsolicited e-mail. It's become a huge business, primarily because it is so easy and cost-effective to send simultaneous messages to millions of people. Some look very personalized, and others look as if they were sent to you accidentally. But keep in mind that spam is never accidental. It's a marketing tool, not objective information. Some spam will offer you the "opportunity" to buy into IPOs or investments. It's a good idea to stay away.

◆ **Unsolicited mail.** If you sign up for magazines or on-line journals, you are likely to be put on a variety of mailing lists. In order to promote their IPOs, small companies will purchase these lists and send out very professional, glossy marketing materials. In most cases, a company has hired a PR firm that knows how to hide the negative and hype the positive. These may actually be "pump and dump" offerings—when a company's officers issue large amounts of stock to brokers, creating the illusion that the stock has done a successful offering, as the price soars. The brokers, in turn, will dump the stock on clients.

As with spam, buyer beware.

◆ **Cold calls.** Cold calls are a key part of the brokerage business. It's called "dialing for dollars." These brokers are playing a numbers game. The more calls they make, the more people will put their money into the "hot" investments they are selling. By far, cold calling is the most cost-effective means of marketing. To be successful, there needs to be only a 1 to 2 percent closure rate.

In most instances, you simply don't want to buy what cold callers are selling. Remember this: If it were such a hot investment they wouldn't be selling it unsolicited over the telephone. Don't ever buy IPO shares over the telephone.

But cold callers can be very convincing. They spend hours every day making the same calls, using the same script. If you want to reduce the number of calls you receive, ask the broker to put you on the Don't Call list, or write a letter to the compliance officer of the firm.

Now that we've explored where to look and where not to look for the latest IPOs and their fundamentals, let's turn to the one information resource all investors need to read before buying any IPO: the prospectus.

CHAPTER

4

Making
SENSE OF THE
PROSPECTUS

OST OF THE specifics you need to evaluate an IPO are contained in its prospectus. The company is required by law to disclose all material information—the good, the bad and often times, the ugly. It's all in there.

There are several ways to get a copy of the prospectus. The easiest way, as discussed in Chapter 3, is to download the document free from Hoover's IPO Central site or from the SEC's Web site. Your other option is to call the lead underwriter and request that a copy of the preliminary prospectus, or "red herring" be mailed to you, or you can call the company itself and request a copy. Prospectuses are not hard to come by; reading them, on the other hand, is another matter altogether.

Reading a prospectus is not like browsing through your favorite entertainment variety magazine; it's lengthy, full of jargon, and laden with charts and graphs. And here's the worst part—it's written by a lawyer.

But, as daunting as it appears, you don't need an advanced degree to understand this document. Remember: The prospectus is crucial, but you don't have to read all of it. There are a variety of sections that have very little bearing on the IPO investment. For example, many prospectuses contain the lease agreement for the company's facilities. This is something you can skip.

This chapter focuses exclusively on the sections of the prospectus that are most important to investors.

As you continue reading prospectuses, the process will get easier and faster. But, like anything else, it takes practice. As you read through this chapter, it's a good idea to have a sample prospectus (from www.edgar-online.com) in front of you to look at as the pertinent sections are described here.

GOOD NEWS FOR INVESTORS

THE SEC HAS recently adopted what is called "plain English" rules for drafting prospectuses. These rules require that the cover pages, the summary, and the risk factors sections be easy to understand, for obvious reasons. Basically, the issuer must comply with these three rules (which are now in effect):

1 short sentences with definite, concrete, everyday language

2 active, rather than passive, voice

3 bulleted lists for complex information; absolutely no legal jargon; and no multiple negatives.

To help promote plain English rules, the SEC vows that it will delay the approval for registration statements and prospectuses that do not comply. This happy development will make it much easier to analyze an IPO prospectus in the future.

A prospectus usually has between twenty and thirty sections. These are the most common ones investors should expect to see:

1 Front page

2 Prospectus Summary

3 The Company

4 Summary Consolidated Financial Data

5 Risk Factors

6 Use of Proceeds

7 Dividend Policy

8 Dilution

9 Capitalization

10 Selected Consolidated Financial Data

11 Management's Discussion and Analysis of Financial Condition and Results of Operations

12 Business

13 Management

14 Certain Transactions

15 Principal Stockholders

16 Description of Capital Stock

17 Shares Eligible for Future Sale

18 Certain United States Federal Tax Considerations for Non-U.S. Holders of Common Stock

19 Underwriters

20 Legal Matters

21 Experts

22 Additional Information

23 Index to Consolidated Financial Statements

The remainder of this chapter explains the portions of the Prospectus that IPO investors need to understand and to focus on.

FRONT PAGE

THE FIRST SECTION of the prospectus is called the "front page." And yes, it all fits on one page. This is where you'll find some basic reference information on the company and, more specifically, on the offering. You'll see the type of offering it is, such as an S-1 or SB-2. (These offering types are described on page 35 in Chapter 2.) You will also find the address of the company, the names of the managing underwriters, and the exchange that the stock is expected to list on. As you read through the Front Page, you'll see that it contains a table called the *Calculation of Registration Fee*. It looks like this one in the box below, which is from the prospectus of the March 1998 IPO of Internet Services Systems (ISS).

The Calculation of Registration Fee table contains important information: the estimated share price of the

CALCULATION OF REGISTRATION FEE

	INITIAL PUBLIC OFFERING PRICE	UNDERWRITING DISCOUNT TO COMPANY	PROCEEDS
Per share	$22.00	$1.54	$20.46
Total proceeds to selling shareholders	$66,000,000	$4,620,000	$54,935,100
Per share	$20.46		
TOTAL	$6,444,900		

offering. In ISS's case, that price is listed as $22.00. But when a company first files its prospectus, the initial public offering price is usually stated as a range, because it may take a few months until the stock is eligible to be sold to the public. For example, when ISS filed its original prospectus on January 20, 1998, the proposed offering price was $11. On March 23, 1998, when the company actually did the IPO, the offering price was $22. What's more, during this period, the number of shares to be offered increased from 2,8750,000 to 3,000,000.

You will also see footnotes listed on the Front Page. One common footnote describes the *over-allotment option.* This allows the underwriter to issue additional shares during the IPO, which is exercised if there is heavy demand for the offering. In the case with the ISS offering, the underwriter has the option of purchasing 450,000 more shares than the maximum being offered. The underwriters have thirty days to exercise this option.

As you read further down the front page of the prospectus, you will see how many shares the founders and officers are selling. In the case of ISS, the total was 315,000 shares, amounting to $6,444,900. This may sound like a lot of money, but for an offering of this size, it is a small number. However, if you see an IPO in which the founders and officers sell 30 percent or more of the amount being offered, it may mean that they are bailing out: In other words, these individuals may not believe in the long-term viability of their company but want to get as much cash as

STANDARD SEC DISCLAIMER

THESE SECURITIES HAVE NOT been approved or disapproved by the Securities and Exchange Commission or any state securities commission nor has the Securities and Exchange Commission or any state securities commission passed upon the accuracy or adequacy of this prospectus. Any representation to the contrary is a criminal offense.

possible on the day of the offering. This should be a red flag for IPO investors.

It's important to remember that all prospectuses contain the disclaimer at left on the Front Page. In other words, the SEC will not advise whether the offering is a good or bad investment; it's not in the business of recommending stocks. It is up to you to decide if the investment has potential. The SEC simply maintains that the company has complied with the securities laws, such as disclosing the necessary information in the right format.

QUALIFICATION REQUIREMENTS

IN SOME PROSPECTUSES, but not all, you'll see a section just before the Prospectus Summary that's known as qualification requirements.

Investors beware. Qualification requirements mean that a state or the SEC deems the offering to be risky, and that only high-net-worth individuals may participate. Such a restriction can have a severely negative impact on an offering. If you see qualification requirements, you'll know that an IPO is a particularly high-risk investment.

THE COMPANY

THE COMPANY SECTION runs from five to ten paragraphs or longer. In it, you will find a description of the company and its products and services. For example, ISS's IPO prospectus stated, "the company develops technology to protect Internet networks for companies and governments. It has over 1,500 customers, including nine of the ten largest banks."

The Company section may also contain various surveys or research reports illustrating the market size for the company's products, and its target audience. This section is a *must-read* for investors. It's always important to understand the business a company is in before investing in its IPO.

In the last paragraph of the Company section, you will see the state in which the company is incorporated. In most cases, it will be Delaware. But take note that if the company is incorporated in an offshore haven, such as the Bahamas, investors need to be very wary. The reason for such offshore incorporations is to make it difficult for the SEC to enforce its laws against the company.

RISK FACTORS

THE FACT THAT a prospectus lists risks doesn't, in itself, mean that the IPO is a bad investment. In fact, a prospectus that fails to list any risks would probably never receive SEC approval. After all, by nature investments are never entirely free from uncertainty. Chapter 5 goes into greater detail on some of the more significant risk factors investors should watch for. Here are some of them in brief:

◆ **History of loan default.** This shows that the company will probably go bankrupt unless it raises money from an IPO. The IPO, in other words, is really an act of desperation.

◆ **Negative gross margins.** This means that the company is not likely to make money for quite some time, if ever.

◆ **Recent transition to a new business.** This can mean that the company has lost its focus, and does not have clear goals for the future, or that it's moving into a business that it originally was not set up to pursue.

◆ **Legal proceedings.** Lawsuits are difficult to quantify. What's more, lawsuits can drain resources and divert the attention of management away from its business operations.

◆ **Prior unsuccessful offering.** This means that the company had trouble convincing investors to invest in the IPO.

◆ **Inexperienced management team.** Running a public company requires an experienced management team. Managers who are not qualified will cause major problems for the company.

◆ **Product concentration.** Relying on a single product is risky. If the customer base dries up or the product becomes outdated, the impact can be substantial.

◆ **Low priced stocks.** Penny stock IPOs are highly risky. Many of these companies have inexperienced management teams, unproved business models, and little capital with which to expand their business.

USE OF PROCEEDS

AS THE NAME implies, the "Use of Proceeds" section indicates exactly what a company intends to do with the money it raises in the IPO. In many cases, this section is vague. However, investors should look for certain things. For example, you will often see an estimation of how long the company will survive on the infusion of IPO capital. In most cases, it is more than one year—but keep in mind that this is only a guess. Many things can happen to a company, good and bad. If more than 50 percent of the proceeds from an IPO are earmarked for outstanding debts, chances are that the company has dismal growth prospects.

DIVIDENDS

FOR THE MOST PART companies that do IPOs don't pay dividends. The reason is that most of them will invest the IPO capital back into their operations in order to accelerate growth.

But there are some industries that do pay dividends. Real Estate Investment Trusts (REITs), for example, are required by law to distribute at least 95 percent of their annual taxable income to shareholders in the form of dividends. Other industries that pay dividends include banks and insurance companies.

On occasion, you will see a major dividend distribution when the IPO is initiated. This is always a one-time event with the purpose of providing liquidity for the owners of the company who, in most cases, founded the business years ago and are using the opportunity to cash in. It is understood that the company founders should reap the benefit of their efforts and vision, but sometimes that compensation can go too far.

DILUTION

DILUTION IS THE difference between what existing share-holders (founders) and new shareholders (investors) will pay for shares. The existing shareholders usually pay a much lower price for the stock than IPO investors do. Dilution is common in all IPOs. However, sometimes it can be excessive.

A reasonable number to look for in the prospectus is 60 to 70 percent dilution. Anything much higher than that can signal a problem for investors.

SELECTED QUARTERLY FINANCIAL RESULTS

A CHART SHOWING the income statement data broken down on a quarterly basis can indicate developing company trends. However, keep in mind that some of the quarterly data can be misleading. For example, a bad quarter may be the result of a cyclical factor and not an indication of the deterioration of the company. So, if you are looking at fourth quarter results, compare them to the fourth quarter of the prior year instead of other quarters. Quarter-to-quarter results are most accurate. And, try to read the meaning between the numbers. If you see a dramatic drop or increase, make it your business to know the reason behind it.

LIQUIDITY AND CAPITAL RESOURCES

AS THE OLD SAYING goes, "Cash is king." Without it, you have no company. "This is one of the first things I look at," says Mark Spitzer, President of FreeEDGAR, "I want to see where the company is getting its money and how it is spending it."[2] The "Liquidity and Capital Resources" section shows how much a company is spending—and on what areas of the business—as well as how much money is in the bank.

ACCOUNTING STANDARDS

WHEN READING THE financial data, you will see the acronym GAAP, which stands for Generally Accepted Accounting Principles. GAAP rules are the standard procedures that accountants abide by when preparing accounting statements. These standards are derived from an organization called the Financial Accounting Standards Board (FASB).

BUSINESS

THE "BUSINESS" SECTION is a comprehensive description of the company, including a succinct summary of the business, size of the market, company products and services, a description of R&D, the number of employees, and a list of top customers. You'll also read about marketing initiatives and office space.

MANAGEMENT

THIS SECTION LISTS the senior managers of the company and the board members. Each will be described in a one-paragraph resume. As indicated earlier in this chapter, look for management that has prior experience running public companies. Be careful of companies that have a senior manager who currently works for or used to be part of the investment bank that is managing the IPO. Such management may be more concerned about engaging in financial shenanigans to line their pockets than in running the company for the long term. At the very least, there is the potential for conflicts of interest.

Also be cautious of companies that have senior managers who are related to each other. If the CFO is the twenty-four-year-old son of the founder/CEO, the company could run into trouble.

CERTAIN TRANSACTIONS

THIS SECTION SHOWS the history of the financing of the company, including the involvement of angel investors and venture capitalists. Look for those companies that have angels with strong industry experience. And look for VCs with good track records.

On occasion, you will see some evidence of conflicts of interest. For example, the company may have lent money to some of the senior officers. Or, the company may be doing business with a firm owned by a senior manager. Thus, the company may not get the best deal, which could hurt shareholder value.

SHARES ELIGIBLE FOR FUTURE SALE

SIX MONTHS AFTER a successful IPO, you may see the stock suddenly fall, say 10 or 20 percent, without any apparent reason. The cause of such a sell-off may be that the lock-up period has expired and company insiders are cashing in some of their stake.

A lock-up provision, disclosed in this section of the prospectus, gives control of a company's stock to the underwriters for a limited period of time. Essentially, venture capitalists, founders, and senior executives are restricted from selling their stock for about 120 to 180 days to prevent major selling pressure.

When the lock-up period expires, however, the holders of the stock may want to start selling, especially if the stock has increased a great deal and appears to be overvalued. Investors should be aware of the lock-up expiration date, and realize that they may see some shares changing hands and some price movement.

INDEX TO CONSOLIDATED FINANCIAL STATEMENTS

THIS LAST SECTION of the prospectus includes the full financial statements of the company. You don't need to get your calculator recharged right this second, but for those readers who are mathematically inclined, Appendix B on page 234 contains some handy analysis techniques.

However, we will take a look now at how financial statements are structured. First, let's go to the income statement, which shows the company's sales (revenues) and expenses over a period of time. The difference between these two numbers is called *Income Before Income Taxes*. After you subtract the taxes, the remaining amount is called net income—that is, profit.

INCOME STATEMENT

THIS IS WHAT you'll see on the income statement:

◆ **Revenues.** This includes all the money the company has made. These sales are adjusted for any discounts given, and for returns.

◆ **Cost of Goods Sold (COGS).** COGS is the total of financial resources spent to purchase and manufacture the inventory to be sold to customers. COGS is applicable for only product companies. If the company sells services, it will have cost of services.

◆ **Operating Expenses.** These include Research and Development, Sales and Marketing, and General and Administrative.

◆ **General & Administrative.** These costs are for salaries for executives, sales personnel, support services, and professional services fees such as for legal work.

◆ **Revenues or Gains.** These are items that are not within the normal, continuing operations of the company, such as when a company decides to sell a subsidiary.

◆ **Other Expenses or Losses.** These are expenses or losses that are not within the normal, continuing operations of the company. Again, this is a one-time transaction.

◆ **Pretax Income from Continuing Operations.** This is the difference between the Operating Net Income and the other revenues and expenses.

◆ **Income Taxes.** Discloses taxes paid. If a company has losses, it will not have to pay income taxes.

◆ **Net Income.** This is the pretax income minus income taxes.

BALANCE SHEET

NEXT, YOU WILL SEE balance sheet information. Essentially, a balance sheet lists company assets, liabilities, and equity. Assets are listed on the basis of their historical cost; market value appreciation in value is not accounted. For example, suppose a company purchased real estate for $1 million. Five years later, the real estate might be worth $3 million. The asset will still be listed on the balance sheet at $1 million.

The following are the most common asset items on a balance sheet (they are usually listed in order of liquidity):

◆ **Current assets.** These are short-term and can be converted into cash within one year. Examples include:

CASH. This is money in a bank account.

MARKETABLE SECURITIES. Stocks, bonds, and other securities.

ACCOUNTS RECEIVABLE. This includes the amount of money that customers owe the company. Often, you will see an item called *Allowance for Doubtful Accounts,* which is an estimate of how much money the company believes it will be unable to collect from customers.

INVENTORIES. These include the work in process, raw materials, and merchandise used in the manufacturing and selling operations.

PREPAID EXPENSES. These are expenses for services that a company has paid for but has yet to receive. Examples: prepaid rent, prepaid insurance.

◆ **Noncurrent assets.** These are assets that can be converted into cash after at least one year. Examples include:

LONG-TERM INVESTMENTS. Stocks, bonds, and other securities that will be held for the long term. However, to be classified as long term, the company must have a significant stake in the stock or bond (usually at least 20 percent).

PROPERTY, PLANT, AND EQUIPMENT. Long-term assets

such as the land, machinery, tools, buildings used in the normal course of business. You will typically see another item called Accumulated Depreciation. Depreciation is a method a company uses to expense long-term assets.

NATURAL RESOURCES. Resources such as oil, gas, minerals, or timber that can be extracted from the ground. When these resources are removed, the company will deduct the value of the natural resources item by a process called depletion.

INTANGIBLE ASSETS. These are nonphysical, long-term assets. Examples include copyrights, patents, franchises, trademarks, trade names, and goodwill. Goodwill is the excess of the cost of an acquired company over the its book value.

LIABILITIES INCLUDE BOTH current and noncurrent items:

◆ **Current liabilities.** Debts that must be paid within one year. Examples include:

ACCOUNTS PAYABLE. Money a company owes its suppliers.

CURRENT MATURITIES OF LONG-TERM DEBT. Expenses related to long-term debt. For example, suppose a company has a mortgage for $10 million that is payable over ten years. The current year's interest payment will be listed in this category.

UNEARNED REVENUES. Revenues that have been collected in advance, such as magazine subscription revenues.

ACCRUED EXPENSES. Money owed for taxes, payrolls, and other expenses.

◆ **Noncurrent liabilities.** These are debts with payments extending beyond one year.

CONTINGENT LIABILITIES. Money a company may potentially owe for things like pending litigation. The company will estimate the amount of this liability.

DEFERRED INCOME TAXES. A difference between the numbers on the company's financial statements and the numbers reported on the income tax statement. The method to calculate a company's financial statements and income taxes are usually different. Thus, this difference will represent a liability to the U.S. government.

LEASES. A capital lease is reported on the balance sheet. That is, the company is essentially getting complete ownership of the property through the lease. However, if this is not the case, then the company has an operating lease, which is not reported on the balance sheet. Look for it in the footnotes.

LONG-TERM DEBT. Mortgages and notes.

◆ **Equity.** Equity is the difference between the total assets and liabilities. So, if the company has $30 million in assets and $20 million in liabilities, the equity is $10 million. Thus, this $10 million is the ownership interest in the company.

These are some components of equity:

CAPITAL STOCK. The par value of the stock issued. This value is stated on the stock certificate and is an arbitrary value; that is, a nominal amount (such as 0.001 cent). The stock is either common stock or preferred stock.

PAID-IN CAPITAL. The excess of the capital stock.

RETAINED EARNINGS. The profits that have been reinvested back into the company. Although, it is more typical that a company has negative retained earnings (since early-stage companies usually lose money). This is known as an *accumulated deficit.*

TREASURY STOCK. Stock that a company has bought back. Since an IPO has never traded on the market, the Treasury Stock item does not apply. Convertible Preferred stock shows the amount of money investors put into the company.

CONCLUSION

CONGRATULATIONS TO THE reader. You have just made your way through the most important parts of an IPO prospectus. Remember: The prospectus is an investor's best friend. It contains most of the information you need to make your investment decision. Chapter 5 goes into more detail on some of the risk factors you might see in the prospectus. Knowing what the risks are is important; realizing what they might mean to your investments is vital.

CHAPTER

Risk
FACTORS

B Y LAW, A company must clearly list in its prospectus all potential risk factors for investors: company situations or industry conditions that might negatively impact the future of the business and the stock price. All investments have risks. What's important, though, is to be able to identify those that might cause trouble for the IPO. These are some of the risk factors you might spot in an IPO prospectus that warrant further consideration:

INEXPERIENCED MANAGEMENT TEAM

IT IS CRITICAL FOR a company to have a management team that knows how to deal with business complexities that might arise. A recently hired team is one risk factor warranting careful consideration.

Peritus Software Services is a company that develops software and provides services to improve the productivity and quality of the information technology systems of companies. In 1996, Peritus released a product, called the AutoEnhancer/2000, which deals with the Year 2000 problem.

The company grew from $7.8 million in sales in 1994 to $19.2 million in 1996, and the number of employees increased from 130 to 229. But with this growth came some problems worth noting. In 1997 when Peritus initiated an IPO, members of the company's senior management had been with the company less than one year and had limited experience in managing public companies. The top-line underwriter, NationsBanc Montgomery Securities handled the May 1997 IPO. Shares were issued at $16 per share, raising $44.8 million. The stock is now (as of December 1998) selling for $1.

Inexperience within the management team isn't the only reason the stock price is flat, but it certainly has a bearing on the performance of any company.

LEGAL PROCEEDINGS

ANOTHER RISK FACTOR worth investigating is serious litigation pending against the company. The problem with litigation is that it is difficult to quantify. After all, it is almost impossible to know how a jury will decide a case, or how much it will award a company in damages. What's more, a protracted lawsuit can divert a company's attention and resources away from its focus.

Some interesting examples of this include:

◆ **Shopping.com.** In July 1997 a former consultant to the company filed a lawsuit alleging that it failed to pay agreed-upon compensation, which was fully disclosed in the prospectus. The SEC, as a result of the litigation, suspended trading of the stock for a week.

◆ **Jenna Lane.** Founded in 1995, the company designs, manufactures and markets sportswear for women. Several people associated with management had run-ins with the law. The president and co-CEO was convicted in state court for larceny. In addition to this, Stanley Kaplan, who helped promote the stock offering of Jenna Lane, signed a consent decree with the SEC for securities violations. All of this was disclosed in the prospectus. Jenna Lane went public in March 1997, raising $6.1 million. The offering price was $10.13. The stock currently sells for $2.50.

Also, be wary of any disclosures of legal problems involving the underwriter. In certain states, an underwriter having been banned from financial activities can definitely stunt the offering.

MARKET AND CUSTOMER BASE

AN IDEAL CANDIDATE for IPO investment is a company with a potentially large, fast-growing market. This sounds obvious, but not all IPO candidates are lucky enough or are designed to have diverse product offerings.

Product concentration can be a major problem for young businesses. A company may have only a few products, sometimes just one. And, if such a company's singular product hits a sales slump, it can lead to overall under-performance for the company and its stock.

Reliance on a small number of customers, similar to product concentration, limits potential for growth and chances to recover in an evolving, competitive market-place. Be careful of a company that sells its products to only a few customers.

An example is ASD Group Inc. This company provides contract manufacturing and engineering services to original equipment manufacturers, such as GE and IBM. However, 71 percent of net sales are derived from four customers. In December 1996, two of the company's largest customers temporarily reduced shipment levels. The company went public at $5.75 in May 1997, raising about $6 million. The stock is now selling for only $1.

TECHNOLOGY RISK

THERE HAS BEEN a lot of press regarding the Year 2000 Problem (also known as *Y2K*); and the SEC has taken notice, indicating that companies must make necessary disclosures of the problems and the costs of resolving them.

Y2K, which can affect almost any type of company, has its origins in the days of mainframe computers. At that time there was not much memory for programmers to work with. As a result, they developed software that was very efficient at the expense of longevity. One method was to have dates represented by two digits. This system works for dates in the twentieth century, but it fails when dealing with the twenty-first century. If the problem isn't rectified, the dates built into various computer systems will revert to 1900 when the new millennium begins.

In many cases, correcting Y2K problems that are imbedded into inventory systems, accounts payable networks, and many other programs is labor-intensive and expensive. For the most part, programmers must look at software systems line-by-line. It is estimated that industry will pay several hundred billion dollars to solve the problem.

If this or another technology-related problem exists in a company you are researching, make sure you know how much resolving it will cost. Is the extent of the problem difficult to quantify? The key word to look for in the prospectus is material. That is, will the problem have a measurable impact on the company? If the problem is very serious, you might want to stay away from the IPO.

NEGATIVE GROSS MARGINS

THINK TWICE BEFORE investing in any company that has negative gross margins. It's possible that such a company will never be profitable.

Rockwell Medical Technologies (RMTI) is an example of this scenario. The company develops hemodialysis concentrates and dialysis kits. Unfortunately, the company's cost structure has resulted in huge losses. Since its inception, the company has had a gross margin deficit of $391,119, primarily the result of the company's massive transportation costs—it has its own trucking operations.

As Rockwell's prospectus states: "There can be no assurance that the company will ever operate." This is a very serious statement to see in the Risk Factors section of any prospectus.

Rockwell's stock was offered at $4 per share. The stock is now selling at $2. And, since the IPO, the company has continued to incur negative gross margins.

LIMITED HISTORY OF
PROFITABLE OPERATIONS

IT TAKES TIME to build profitable operations. In its early stages, a company will spend a lot of money developing its infrastructure, products and market share. However, over time, the company should be able to reach critical mass and achieve profitability. In fact, raising capital through an IPO should help accelerate the process of reaching critical mass, but it takes time.

Most Internet companies, for example, have big losses in their early years. However, many high-tech businesses that have gone public have recorded strong revenue growth and rapidly growing markets. Wall Street is expecting that, over the next several years, these companies will become profitable, and because of this forecast, Internet company IPOs have had the best performance of any sector in the first half of 1998. So, just because a company is unprofitable for the short-term does not mean the IPO will fail. Rather, the key factor is that the expected future growth rate should be high.

However, be wary of those companies that describe long-term losses—over ten years or more. This is a strong indication that the business will never be profitable.

SkyMall is an example of an IPO with long-term losses. If you've flown on an airline, you've seen Skymall's catalogs, which are located in the front pockets of each passenger seat. The catalog is chock-full of premium (that is, expensive) goods from Disney and The Sharper Image. In fact, The SkyMall has about 70 percent of the market for domestic passengers or 960,000 passengers each day.

Prior to going public the company had impressive revenue growth. From 1991 to 1995, sales grew from $5.4 million to $43.1 million, while sales per passenger increased from $0.038 to $0.084. Despite this growth, the company was unable to generate any profits. The gross margins were small because of high distribution and printing costs and low mark-ups. In fact, the company had accumulated losses of $32.4 million.

The Skymall went public on December 1996. The amount raised was $16 million and the offering price was $8 per share. Since then, the company has been a dismal performer. The stock is trading at about $4. By reading the Risk Factors, it would have been easy to spot this company's long string of losses.

You may also find a company that has a long history of erratic earnings. This is the case with Celerity Systems. The company designs, develops, integrates and installs interactive video services hardware and software, as well as CD-ROM software products for business applications.

Founded in 1993, the Celerity Systems incurred losses of $264,000 the first year. In 1994, the company lost $30,000 and, in 1995, generated profits of $9,900. Then, in 1996, the company had a huge loss of $5.5 million. For the first six months of 1997, the company had losses of $3.8 million. The Risk Factors in the company's IPO prospectus indicated that the company reserved about $570,000 for uncollectable accounts receipts and $673,000 for uncompleted contracts. Also disclosed were problems with a major customer, reluctant to pay its bills.

Even with this questionable earnings pattern, Hampshire Securities took the company public in November 1997 at $7.50 per share, raising $15 million. The stock now sells for $4.50.

UNSUCCESSFUL PRIOR PUBLIC OFFERING

ON OCCASION, AN IPO will fail. A company will file its registration statement to go public, but will then pull the offering from the market, usually because there is little demand for the stock. (Investors do not lose money in such a situation because the stock is not sold.) Perhaps the market environment is bad or the company is slipping. That same company may, after a year or two, try again to complete an IPO. Be careful with companies that try repeat IPOs; they can be very risky investments.

One example is ThermaCell Technologies. The company originally tried a "best efforts" offering in 1996, attempting to sell a minimum of 833,333 shares at $6 per share. But the IPO failed because the company was unable to generate enough demand for the stock (investors were skeptical of the company's prospects). All investor funds had to be returned. Because of the expenses of the failed offering, the company had to close its Florida sales office, vacate its executive offices, reduce significantly its marketing plans and lay off employees. The company also defaulted on its $505,000 bridge loan.

Despite these problems, the company was able to return

to the capital markets and do an IPO again in 1997, raising $5.5 million. The offering price was $4. Now, the stock is selling for about $2.

The original failed attempt of the IPO was not the only reason for the latter failure. There were other reasons, such as poor operating performance of the company. However, the fact that the company had a failed attempt at an IPO was a strong indication that serious problems existed.

COMPETITION

COMPETITION IS MENTIONED in every prospectus. It is the nature of business as we know it. In fact, the presence of competition can be positive because it indicates that there is a market for the company's products or services.

However, sometimes competition can be extremely fierce, particularly in fast-paced industries like technology. In any case, it's a potential risk factor that investors need to be aware of. Reading the Competition section of the prospectus can give investors a very good idea of the various players in the industry that are vying for market share.

An interesting example is Netscape, the company which we know developed the ubiquitous Netscape Navigator Internet browser. Of course, its main competitor was and still is the giant Microsoft, which has squashed many other potentially competitive companies.

If you read Netscape's prospectus for its 1995 IPO, you would clearly see risks of competition stated. The prospectus indicated that Microsoft Corporation expressed its intentions to improve and bundle its browser (called Explorer) to its Windows 95 operating system. It also says that: "While the anticipated penetration of this software into Microsoft's installed base of PC users will increase the size and usefulness of the Internet, it will likely also have a material adverse impact on Netscape's ability to sell client software."

Netscape had a very strong performance on its opening and then continued to do well. However, the stock reached a peak at $78.98. The stock is now selling for $38. Microsoft stock, on the other hand, has soared since the Netscape IPO, going from $21 to $128. Netscape recently merged with AOL in order to compete against Microsoft.

The moral here is that some competition is more dangerous than others.

RISK OF LOW-PRICED STOCK

IF A STOCK is offered at below $5 per share, then, according to SEC regulations it is considered a "penny stock". Penny stocks, as noted in Chapter 2, are extremely risky and, for the most part, not appropriate for individual investors. Their chances for long-term success are questionable.

DEFAULT ON OUTSTANDING INDEBTEDNESS

IT IS COMMON for a company to borrow money prior to an IPO. But, default on such a debt is an indication that the company suffers from poor cash management. Since a default has a material impact on the company, it is mentioned in the prospectus.

One such company is Marine Management Systems. The company develops, markets, and sells software for the communications systems of commercial ships in the international maritime industry. Marine has twenty-seven years of experience in the industry and a large customer base of 1,500 installations. Despite this, Marine was spending huge amounts of cash before its IPO. By the time of its offering in May 1997, the company had a negative working capital deficit of $1.8 million.

The company had to borrow large sums of money to feed the spending, a debt which was backed by the assets of the company. Thus, in the event of a default, the bank would have legal title to the company. But when the company did violate certain loan covenants, it was able to obtain a waiver for the violations.

When you see a company with problems in its debt

structure, be extremely careful. It is likely to be an investor time bomb. Marine went public at $5 per share, raising $7 million. The stock now sells at five cents.

RECENT TRANSITION TO A NEW BUSINESS MODEL

IT CAN BE SCARY when a company decides to get into a new business—especially within, say, a year or so of its IPO. This makes it difficult to analyze the business, since its prior history is not good guide to the future. What's more, it is never easy to completely change the direction of a business. Such a process is fraught with risks, for the company and for its investors.

One such example is Qualix Group. The company was originally a distributor, value-added reseller, and publisher of client/server software products. The company then, in 1993, entered the quality assurance business, introducing a product called QualixHA for the Unix operating system. By 1996, the company took another turn by merging with Octopus Technologies. Now the company develops remote data mirroring products for the Windows NT operating system.

Perhaps this partly explains why the company accumulated $6.5 million in losses since its founding in 1990. It went public in February 1997. The offering was priced at $8.50. The stock is now trading at $3.

These are just some of the risk factors you'll come across while reading the IPO prospectus. There are other legal, financial, industry, and business risks that also come into play with any investment. The severity of many of these risks depends largely upon the nature of the company and how that specific risk will affect it in the future. If a prospectus is full of seemingly serious risk factors, reconsider the investment. Or, at least educate yourself further on the risks that are listed.

CHAPTER 6

IPO
INVESTMENT
STRATEGIES

LL GREAT INVESTORS have philosophies that direct their trading. Warren Buffet, for example, looks for stocks that have strong brand names, substantial market share, and top-notch managements; the famous Peter Lynch's philosophy is similar. William Nasgovitz, manager of the Heartland Small-Cap Contrarian Fund, chooses small, domestic stocks that he believes are undervalued. This chapter will describe a variety of common IPO investment strategies. First, we'll examine some simple, commonsense ways to get started in IPOs, then we'll cover some more sophisticated strategies, often better left to the pros.

BASIC STRATEGIES FOR INVESTORS

NEIGHBORHOOD INVESTING

IN SOME CASES, a great IPO might be happening right in your own backyard. Local companies make tempting investment opportunities because you'll have first-hand knowledge about the business and easy access to research. Perhaps you're even a customer who knows the management personally.

At the very least, close proximity to a company that's going public allows you the opportunity to visit the company's operations and make a firsthand judgment of their environment. When you visit its offices, learn as much as you can about its products and staff. For instance:

◆ Do the employees look busy and content?

◆ Is the product good quality? Would you use it?

◆ Are the facilities organized and clean?

While you're there, it is also a good idea to talk to the employees. Get their feedback on what they like about their company. In fact, you may even get easier access to shares in the offering if you get to know some of the people who work there. Visiting the company personally won't provide all the answers you need to invest in an IPO, but it will give you a head start.

Another great source of information on regional companies is the local newspaper. You will typically find in-depth business and feature coverage on local companies, and should even look at the classified ads to see if the company is hiring.

Perhaps one of the best examples of backyard investing is Wal-Mart. The company is now the nation's largest retailer and has made millionaires of thousands of home-town residents of Bentonville, Arkansas. Another example is Home Depot, which went public in 1984, with only thirty-one stores. Yes, this company, too, made many people in its hometown (Atlanta, Georgia) millionaires.

INVEST IN WHAT YOU KNOW

IT'S A GOOD IDEA to invest in the industries that you understand best. If you have insight into the construction business—perhaps because you're a builder or contractor—then chances are you have as much insight into industry trends and performance as the analysts. And you're in a great position to more easily determine the upside of companies in that field.

It's no fluke that doctors don't invest in medical companies. What is it that they know?

In other words, you should consider your own profession and how it will help you invest in IPOs. If you're a banker and understand the dynamics of the financial services industry, it makes sense to look at finance company IPOs. If you work in Silicon Valley, you have a lot of IPOs to choose from.

You can also use your knowledge as a consumer. If you are an avid book buyer, chances are that you wish you had invested in AMAZON.com. If you want to invest in a restaurant IPO, make sure that you dine at that chain. If you are considering an investment in an Internet company, make sure you spend time on the Web site.

Use the knowledge of business you've gained over the

years to spot IPOs with the most potential. Although this is only one of many screens, it's one that everyone can start with.

STUDY MUTUAL FUND HOLDINGS

AS WE'LL DISCUSS in Chapter 12, a variety of mutual funds buy large amounts of IPO shares. One simple strategy for individual investors is to examine the top holdings of such funds. If particular IPOs are good enough for portfolio managers, they might make sense in your personal portfolio, too. There's no telling what ideas you can glean from some of the experts. However, this doesn't exonerate you from engaging in the usual research on the IPOs you discover. After all, even portfolio managers pick lemons.

WATCH WHAT THE ANALYSTS SAY

AFTER A COMPANY goes public, you might notice that several brokerage firms place "buy" recommendations on the stock. It is a good idea to call those brokerage firms to request these reports. Although you shouldn't base your investment decisions solely on this coverage, it's a valuable source of free research.

Keep in mind, too, that in many cases the underwriter will have its own staff of analysts who publish recommendations, too. You can bet that the underwriting firm will have a "buy" on the stock, but it's still worth reviewing their data. And if an analyst who was involved with the offering comes out with a negative recommendation on the stock, this is a serious indication that the company is in trouble.

The bottom line is that it's very useful to review Wall Street's analysis of an IPO, but it's also important to maintain a healthy skepticism regarding their "buy" recommendations.

ANALYSTS' COVERAGE OF IPOS

EVEN IF AN analyst does not have an existing underwriting relationship with the company, you should still remember to be cautious for these reasons:

1 Brokers make their money by getting clients to buy stock.

2 Analysts like high-growth IPOs the most. But high-growth may not be what you, as an investor, are looking for (because high growth often comes with high risk).

3 Analysts sometimes give "buy" recommendations for the wrong reason—to give them better access to the company.

4 Analysts are inclined to give "buy" recommendations in hopes of getting the company as a future client for investment banking services. In fact, it is not uncommon for an analyst to get a referral fee for bringing in investment banking clients.

BUY ON THE OPENING OR . . .
WAIT FOR THE LOCK-UP TO EXPIRE

IF YOU ARE allocated IPO stock at the offering price and it is a hot issue, then it makes sense to participate. A hot issue is an IPO that increases in value immediately upon the effective date of the offering. So, investors holding stock at the opening price have made money immediately.

To spot a hot IPO, look for the following factors:

1 Several days before the IPO, the underwriter increases the price and the number of shares for the offering.

2 Brokers indicate that there are no more shares available.

3 You've heard a good deal of buzz in the press about the IPO.

Buying an IPO at the offering price can mean a very quick profit for investors if their shares are sold quickly. When investors do this, it is known as *flipping*. Underwriters, however, do not look kindly on flipping because it causes price volatility. In fact, they sometimes penalize investors who flip by not offering them shares in a future IPO.

If you are not allocated shares at the opening price of an IPO, the smartest thing to do is to wait.

Steve Harmon, Internet Stock Analyst at Mecklermedia, named by CBS Marketwatch as "one of the Best of Wall Street," says "IPOs are very speculative. And with so much demand on the first day, the price may not immediately be indicative of the company's 'intrinsic' valuation but rather 'instant demand' from buyers. And we all know what happens when demand exceeds supply—inflated prices."[3]

In many cases, an IPO will eventually come back to its offering price at some point in its trading life. The main reason for this is that when a company goes public, there is tremendous excitement. As a result of the hype, the stock will usually jump a great deal. For example, when Broadcast.com went public in July 1998 the stock rose 248 percent on the first day. Investors were excited about the company's Internet video technology. But, as time went by, the hype subsided and so did the stock price.

Unfortunately, there is no scientific formula for buying into an IPO. But here is one sensible approach: Wait six months from the effective date before you buy your shares. This is about the time that the lock-up period expires (as explained in Chapter 6), which means that the officers and founders of the company will be selling shares. This puts undue pressure on the stock, so you may have an opportunity to get it at a very good price.

ADVANCED INVESTMENT STRATEGIES

SHORT SELLING

ALTHOUGH IT SOUNDS almost un-American, you can make money when a stock falls in value by short selling.

Are you a bear in this bull market? And, are you a very sophisticated investor? Then, short selling might be an ideal strategy for you.

In a short sell, you first sell the stock in hopes that it will fall. Once the stock is lower, you will buy it back. That is, the buy/sell process is reversed. How do you sell a stock

first? Basically, you borrow the shares from your broker
and then, later, purchase them in the open market and
return the shares to the broker.

Over the years, short selling has become quite controversial. Perhaps the most notorious short seller of all time
was the legendary trader Jesse Livermore, who became
known as the "King of the Bears." He sold short Union
Pacific Railroad stock one day before the San Francisco
earthquake of 1906, and made a killing in the process.

Then there was Joseph Kennedy, who purportedly
made millions short selling RCA stock (as well as others)
just before the 1929 stock market crash. Add to the list
nefarious Albert Wiggan, the president of Chase Bank,
who sold short the stock of his own company during 1929
and made $4 million.

With this kind of history, short selling has attained a
negative connotation. In fact, you will see occasional statements from CEOs denouncing short sellers as irresponsi-
ble speculators.

Clearly, this is a strategy best reserved for sophisticated
investors. Short selling is actually common in professional
money management circles. Famous investors such as
George Soros and Michael Steinhardt have popularized
the approach. It's a strategy used by many hedge fund
managers. However, it's certainly not the right approach
for everyone.

That said, the IPO market is ripe for short selling. This is
how short-selling works for the IPO investor: Suppose a
company does an IPO and the stock soars from $10 to $20
on the first day of trading. Also suppose that you have reason to believe that price is highly overvalued and that the
stock will collapse. Your next step is to short sell, perhaps,
1,000 shares of the stock at $20. That is, you borrow 1,000
shares from your broker and then sell the stock. This will
net you $20,000, which will then be kept in an escrow
account. However, this is not free. You will have to put up 50
percent of the $20,000 in a margin account. If the stock
increases in value, you are required to put up more margin.

SHORT SELLING

A FAMOUS EXAMPLE of short selling takes us back to the debunked carpet cleaning company, ZZZZ Best, founded in November 1985. The founder of the company, Barry Minkow, was in his early 20s. In 1987, The Feshbach Brothers, investors who specialized in selling short, began to spot some peculiarities with the company. First, ZZZZ Best announced an extraordinary $8 million contract for carpet cleaning of two buildings in Sacramento. After some research, however, the Feshbach Brothers determined that the largest carpet cleaning contracts to date was a mere $3.5 million awarded for cleaning the carpets at the MGM Grand and Las Vegas Hilton. Therefore, the $8 million announcement from Minkow looked like a sham.

The Feshbach brothers took the false contract as a sign that the company was in trouble, so they aggressively shorted the stock—and in the end made a fortune.

ZZZZ Best filed for bankruptcy soon after and Minkow was eventually sentenced to 25 years for securities fraud. It turned out that ZZZZ Best had no revenues at all but was instead a money-laundering scheme.

You don't have to uncover criminal fraud to short a stock; however, you should have a good reason to believe the stock price is about to drop in value.

What's more, if you sell stock short on the NYSE, AMEX, or Nasdaq, you must make the transaction on an "up tick"; that is, the stock must have increased in value. This is to help prevent undue sales pressure on the stock.

According to the short-sale agreement with any firm, you will need to return eventually the 1,000 shares to the brokerage firm. Let's suppose the stock does collapse to $5. You will then buy 1,000 shares for $5,000 and return the shares back to the brokerage, thus netting a $15,000 profit. This is called *covering your short position.*

But what if the stock does not fall, and instead soars to $50. You will need to spend $50,000 to buy back your stock in order to cover your short position. Suppose the stock goes to $90 or $150. In fact, there is really no limit to how much money you can lose in a short sale. It is no surprise that there are many investors who have gone bankrupt from short selling.

As you can see, short selling can be very risky, especially in an offering, because IPO stock can soar to great heights. For example, Onsale.com went public at $6 per share and then quickly fell to $3. Suppose you shorted the stock at $6 but did not cover it at $3. The stock then soared to $32. That would have cost you $260,000 if you had sold 10,000 shares.

If you decide to sell short stock, don't do so merely because a stock has increased or decreased substantially in value. Rather, you must do in-depth analysis of the company and determine a concrete reason to think that the price is about to collapse.

Factors to consider before selling short include:

◆ Significant selling of shares from the company officers and founders
◆ Continually deteriorating profit margins
◆ Escalating debt levels
◆ Fierce competition
◆ Inexperienced underwriter
◆ Prior violations of securities laws of the company managers
◆ Inexperienced managers
◆ Going concern audit
◆ Expiration of the lock-up period
◆ Developmental stage of the company
◆ Few market makers in the stock
◆ Major break in the stock price
◆ Excessive trading volume, such as, at least twice the daily average.

BUYING ON MARGIN

MARGIN (ALSO CALLED *buying on margin*) is when you purchase a stock with money that's borrowed from a broker. It should be noted that buying IPOs on margin only magnifies the risk that comes with the investment.

In fact, one of the reasons for the famous stock market crash of 1929 was the widespread use of margin (which, at the time, was unlimited and unregulated). It wiped out many wealthy investors of the day. Although margin accounts have been fairly lucrative during bull markets, they become very dangerous in bear markets.

For the most part, the interest rates on margin loans are very competitive (and much better than most credit cards). But keep in mind: This interest can slowly eat away at your portfolio.

For example, suppose you have a $100,000 portfolio of stocks. You can borrow another $100,000 on margin and buy 10,000 shares of Onsale.com IPO at $10 each. In five months, if the stock skyrockets to $20, you will have made another $100,000.

But, let's suppose the stock falls to $2 per share. Your portfolio of Onsale.com is now worth $20,000. However, all brokerage firms have a minimum maintenance margin, from 25 percent to 30 percent of the original amount borrowed—in this case $25,000 to $30,000. Since the current value of the portfolio is below the minimum maintenance margin, you will have a margin call. This means the broker will require you to put up more cash or securities to increase the portfolio to meet the minimum maintenance margin or the stock in the portfolio will be sold off. Buying IPOs on margin is very tempting, but just like short selling, it can be extremely dangerous.

CONCLUSION

PERHAPS THE BEST piece of advice to take away from this chapter, and this book, is to avoid getting caught up in the hype that often comes with an IPO. It is easy to be lured by the potential for huge gains. But patience is the key. Do your research, study the fundamentals, and wait for the hype to subside. In the end you should get better value.

IMPORTANT IPO
Sectors

PART

II

Technology
IPOs

THE FIRST THING that usually pops into people's minds when they think of IPOs is high-tech companies. This is probably due to the tremendous success in the last few years of the IPOs that have blown through this market. Some serious money has been made in high-tech stocks—the sector that is primarily fueling the U.S. economy.

The world economy is going through an epoch of change comparable to the Industrial Revolution. But instead of wealth being generated with coal, iron, steel, oil, and railroads, the new economy is founded on things on a smaller scale: software, microchips, cell phones, and faxes.

Gordon Moore, a cofounder of Intel, introduced a concept known as Moore's Law which explains the tremendous growth in high tech: the cost of making a semiconductor drops 50 percent every eighteen months. This is the reason why today we can buy a 400 megahertz computer for a less than $2,000.

Moore's Law has an exponential effect on the high-tech industry. For example, as computers multiply, software companies generate a bigger base of customers. It took Microsoft only twenty years to become the second biggest company in the world. As the number of computer sales increases, so does the number of users who have access to the Internet, which helps on-line companies such as Yahoo! and AMAZON.com.

What's more, non-high-tech companies also benefit. They can increase business efficiency and production by purchasing low-priced computers.

Despite the frantic growth in high tech, the industry is still in its early stages. While there are 240 million personal computers in the world, this number is expected to explode to 2.4 billion in ten years. Furthermore, many of these users will also be using the Internet.

It's important to realize, though, that not every investment in a high-tech company is a good one. Here are some general factors to look for to spot the right high-tech companies and their IPOs:

◆ **Continuing research and development.** R&D is absolutely crucial in high-tech growth. Although large expenditures reduce current earnings, over the long-term, R&D can result in tremendous gains. This has been a major factor in the continued growth of such Goliaths as Microsoft, Intel, and Cisco. Intel, for example, spends close to $2 billion annually on R&D.

There are, too, some technology companies that do not need to spend as much money on R&D; such is the case with PC makers, such as Dell and Gateway.

These companies do not develop their own technologies. Rather, they purchase motherboards, graphics cards, and microprocessors, which are used to assemble PCs. But these megacompanies are exceptions. As a general rule, you want to see a company spend at least 7 percent of its revenues on R&D.

Spending the right amount on R&D is not the only factor to check. That money must be spent wisely. One way to gauge the effectiveness of R&D efforts is by examining several years historically. Suppose the company spent $5 million five years ago on R&D to build a product. Was the product released within a few years of that expenditure? And, how did it compare to similar products from the rest of the industry?

◆ **Revolutionizing a traditional business.** If you're lucky enough to spot a company that's truly changing an industry for the better, you've probably found a winner. FedEx revolutionized a very old business, the delivery of packages, by guaranteeing overnight service. AMAZON.com has revolutionized bookselling by bringing its shelves on-line and building a tremendous Web site.

Look for companies that are able to use technology to find high-growth opportunities in mature businesses; these are usually great investments.

◆ **Creating the standard.** A company that becomes a real industry touchstone can essentially capture a market. Qualcomm, for example, distributed a limited edition of its e-mail program, Eudora, over the Internet. Millions of users downloaded the software, and thus made Eudora the standard. Currently, the installed base has over 18 million users. However, the company did not release Eudora until several years after its IPO in 1991.

But Netscape is a company whose IPO benefited greatly from its standard, the Navigator browser. By allowing users to download the software over the Internet, Netscape quickly became a leader in the Internet. About 90 percent of all Internet users had the Navigator browser by 1995. In August of that year, Netscape had one of the biggest IPOs ever, as the stock soared from $28 to $58 on the first day. It eventually reached $157 (prices adjusted at 1996 stock split).

Another company whose IPO was boosted by creating a standard is RealNetworks. This company developed Real Audio and Video, which allows for audio/video on the Web. The company gave its software away but sold its server software (which makes it possible to create the video). In a few years, the company dominated the market

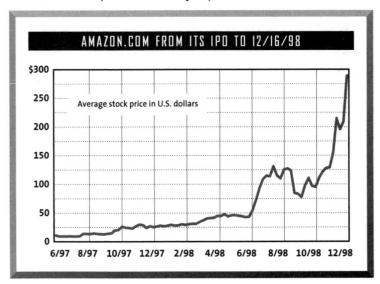

AMAZON.COM FROM ITS IPO TO 12/16/98

SUCCESSFUL SOFTWARE IPOS

◆ **LHS Group.** This company develops client/server billing and customer care software for the telecommunications industry. The technology has been licensed to approximately sixty carriers in over twenty-five countries and supports about 3.5 million subscribers. The company went public in May 1997 at $16 per share. The stock now trades at $57.

◆ **Peregrine.** This company develops service desk software for major corporations. The software works with many diverse systems and helps companies cut the costs of managing their complex computer systems. The company went public in April 1997 at $9 per share. Now, the stock trades at $34.

with an installed base of over 18 million. The company went public in November 1997 at $12.50 per share. The current price is $44.

◆ **Management.** This is a major key in any industry, but particularly in a business that is as high-growth as technology.

Steve Harmon, Internet Stock Analyst at Mecklermedia, says "Overall, I think the most important piece is management. You can pilot the unsinkable ship that brags it cannot be sunk, but how many captains have the humbleness to avert the iceberg? Bill Gates showed he could admit Microsoft was headed the wrong way in 1995—people often overlook that public admittance. What did Microsoft do? It created an iceberg crusher, Internet Explorer, and put 'anti-freeze' in all its applications, including the operating system."[4]

In the remainder of the chapter, we will look at the major segments of the high-tech market which typically create IPOs.

SOFTWARE

SUCCESSFUL SOFTWARE COMPANIES can make you rich. The best performing technology company ever—Microsoft—is, after all, a software company.

The reason for the tremendous gains is that the software industry has a low cost structure. For the most part, the costs are incurred in paying programmers to write code. Once that is done, the company will duplicate CDs (which costs less than a buck) or sell the product from the Internet (which is virtually free of cost). Then it is a matter of marketing the software.

It is not uncommon to see gross profit margins of 90 percent in the software business. Investors love this—and for good reason.

Here's what to look for when hunting for successful software IPOs:

◆ **Cost cutters.** Look for software companies that allow companies to reduce their costs. This was the case with both LHS Group and Peregrine.

◆ **Flexibility.** Make sure that the software can be tailored to particular needs. Is it easy to install? Is it easy to change? What is the pricing structure? What platforms does the software support?

◆ **Products that travel.** There are many opportunities to sell software to foreign companies. However, the software usually needs to be modified for both the language and laws and the regulations of the nation.

◆ **Ability to withstand sales cycle.** Complex software may take several months (or even a year) to sell. The reason is that the software is usually expensive and very comprehensive. A potential customer wants to make sure he is making the right decision. Unfortunately, such long sales cycles can create volatility in revenues and earnings for many software companies.

◆ **Multimarket potential.** Look for software products that can be used for many different markets.

◆ **Strong focus on marketing.** How much money is the

company spending on marketing its products? Having the best technology is not enough—the products also need to sell well.

INTERNET

DURING THE LAST few years, a new industry has emerged and made many investors rich: Internet companies. There is no scientific definition of an Internet company. However, there is the "brick-and-mortar" test: if a company does not have any retail outlets, and instead sells its products exclusively through a Web site, then it is an Internet company. For example, in early 1998, Egghead computer shut down all of its retail outlets to sell its products entirely on the Web.

A second category includes companies like Cisco and Dell. Both sell a tremendous number of their products on the Web. However, the majority of sales are still derived from traditional means with a sales force, advertising, and phone orders.

In the first three quarters of 1998, Internet companies produced more IPOs than any other market sector. From January to November Broadcast.com increased 184 percent, eBay.com increased 544 percent and Earthweb.com increased 240 percent.

But, despite these heady returns, Internet stocks can fall very hard, too. This has been the case with Netscape, which has fallen from the price-adjusted high of $79 in early 1996, to a November 30, 1998 price of $39.

According to Steve Harmon, individuals can successfully invest in Internet stocks as long as they have a strategy and do the prep work. Says Harmon, "The question is: how much time are you willing to invest in researching these companies? If a lot then perhaps it's better to go for the cherry picking method. If little, then go wide—that is, invest in a mutual fund."

Continues Harmon: "In other words, whether investing in mutual funds or individual stocks, it's an advantage to know what the playing field is and who the players are.

SUCCESSFUL INTERNET COMPANY IPOS

◆ **DoubleClick.** This company's technology dynamically delivers targeted, cost-effective, and measurable Internet advertising. DoubleClick has an extensive client list including AltaVista, *US News and World Report, The Wall Street Journal,* and NBC. The company went public February 1998 at $17 per share. The current market price is $36.

◆ **SportsLine USA.** This is a sports-based-content Web site carrying real-time sporting news and merchandise, as well as fantasy leagues. The company also maintains microsites for major sports stars, such as Joe Namath, Shaquille O'Neal, Cal Ripken, Jr., and Wayne Gretzky. The company went public November 1997 at $8 per share. The current price is $25.

Would you bet on the Timbuktu Titans over the Chicago Bulls? If you knew nothing about basketball, you might. If you knew the Titans were a high-school team in way over its head—you wouldn't. But if you also knew the Titans had a 10-foot tall center and three 8-foot guards, you may re-adjust your thinking—and so on. Know your teams and players. Every day on the Internet is a new season."

By any measure, the Internet is one of the fastest growing business sectors on the planet. According to IDC (International Data Corporation), 1997 brought over 29 million Net users in the United States and 50 million users worldwide. By the year 2000, that number is expected to soar to 72 million in the United States and 129 million worldwide. People are spending increasingly more time on the Web. According to a study by the Georgia Institute of Technology, about 51 percent of users access the Web for ten or more hours per week.

Also, people today are buying books, stocks, mortgages, and just about everything else on the Web. An A.C. Nielson study shows that over 20 percent of U.S. Internet users have purchased something on-line. IDC forecasts that on-line purchases will increase from $2.6 billion in 1996 to $220 billion in 2001. This deepening reliance on Internet commerce will continue to multiply profits for Internet companies and investors.

If you are considering investing in Internet IPOs, here's what to look for in the companies:

◆ **Strategic partnerships.** It is important for an emerging company to find new distribution channels and timely content. For example, SportsLine USA successfully partnered with CBS.

◆ **Built-in traffic.** There are several Web sites known as "portals" that serve as destination areas attracting huge amounts of traffic. Examples of portals include search engines, such as Yahoo! and Excite. But, AOL.com is also a portal because of its large user base. To expand business, several Web companies are signing exclusive agreements with such portals to garner their heavy traffic. This is what AMAZON.com, CDNow, Preview Travel, Onsale.com, and other major Web sites have done. These exclusives can be expensive but help upstart Internet companies gain a lot of business quickly.

◆ **Multiple revenue opportunities.** It is very difficult to make profits on the Web. This is why many Internet companies are pursuing multiple revenue options. For example, AMAZON.com had successfully built market share selling books and audio CDs, and it's now branching out with that leg-up into other consumer products.

◆ **Necessities.** When the PC revolution first took the world by storm, there was an immediate need for an operating system. A small company, called Microsoft, provided the solutions with DOS. With the development of the Internet, additional needs presented themselves. For example, electronic commerce requires security measures. VeriSign filled the need by creating digital certificates, on-line identification. VeriSign's IPO was in January 1998 and was priced at $14 per share. It's currently trading at $30.

SUCCESSFUL TELECOM IPOS

◆ **Qwest Communications (QWST).** Qwest is building a huge network of fiber optic lines for major telecom companies, businesses, and consumers (the fibers are state-of-the-art lines manufactured by Lucent Technologies). The network stretches approximately 13,000 route miles coast-to-coast. Qwest did its IPO in June 1997 at $22 per share. The current stock price is $72 (split-adjusted).

◆ **Broadcom (BRCM).** This company develops advanced integrate silicon chips to allow for very fast digital transmissions of data to homes and businesses. The company's technology uses the existing telecom infrastructure. The company offered its IPO in April 1998 at $24 per share. The current stock price is $60.

TELECOMMUNICATIONS

THE SECOND-BEST performing sector in the IPO market in the first half of 1998 was the telecom industry. Although telecom may seem to be at a mature stage in its life cycle, the fact is that only one-third of the world's population has ever used a phone. In other words, the growth potential globally is still huge.

During the past several years, there has been an explosion of voice, data, and video traffic. This has been the result of the spread of technology with PCs, faxes, Internet access, cell phones, and pagers.

To accommodate this growth, the telecom industry has been replacing copper-based lines, which cannot handle large volumes of data, with high-speed digital fiber optic lines. However, much of the new technology has been installed within the existing national infrastructure by telecom behemoths such as WorldCom, MCI, Sprint, and AT&T.

Local connections, however, are still primarily the slower, copper-based variety. This has resulted in what's known as the "last mile" problem or the "bandwidth gap." Top telecom IPOs are the companies that are, in fact, providing solutions for this bandwidth gap. Some of these technologies include digital loop carriers, fiber-to-the-curb, digital subscriber line (xDSL), hybrid fiber coax, and wireless local loop.

Here are some tips for finding successful telecommunications IPOs:

1 Look for companies that can cover their costs. Operating a telecommunications company can be expensive. This is especially the case if the company is constructing a network, such as Qwest is doing. When costly projects are in the plans, make sure the company is raising a large amount of money.

2 Favor businesses with telecom specialization. Telecommunications is extremely complex and specialized. This is why it is important for a telecommunications company to have experienced management. The CEO of Qwest, for example, Joseph Nacchio, was the executive VP of Consumer and the Small Business Division at AT&T, where he worked for twenty-seven years.

3 Focus on companies with strong strategic relationships. It is nearly impossible for a company to do everything (even AT&T cannot). Broadcom, for example, has strategic relationships with 3Com, Bay Networks, Cisco Systems, General Instrument, Motorola, and others.

4 Know who the customers are. If a telecommunications company does not have some major customers, then the technology or network may not be good. For example, Broadcom's customers include Ericsson, Adaptec, Cabletron, Digital Equipment, Nortel, etc.

CONCLUSION

ALTHOUGH THERE ARE many success stories for high-tech IPOs, they do not provide a guaranteed road to riches. In fact, some of the worst-faring IPOs have been high-tech companies. Examples include Scoop (which went bankrupt), USN Communications (dropped 75 percent), and

Aspect Technology (down 65 percent). A company may be king one day and dethroned the next. To invest successfully in high-tech IPOs, you need to actually understand the innovation. It requires a lot of work, but the financial rewards may be worth it.

CHAPTER

Biotech
IPOs

N FEBRUARY 22, 1997, Ian Wilmut made history. In his lab in Scotland, this embryologist created a clone from a mammary gland cell of an adult Dorset sheep. The sheep was appropriately named Dolly.

What was once science fiction is now becoming reality. This is especially true in the field of biotechnology. Biotech is a relatively new industry (dating back only to the mid-1970s). Essentially, biotech develops drugs using the DNA code. There might be, for example, a genetic defect that causes a certain allergy; scientists then endeavor to isolate the defect and to develop a drug to cure the problem.

Although there are many small companies that develop biotech drugs, the major pharmaceutical companies do as well. In fact, the larger companies will typically sign strategic partnerships with biotech firms because it is often the smaller, focused firms that demonstrate the most innovation in developing new drugs. That is, they are not as bogged down with the usual bureaucracy as are the blue-chip pharmaceutical companies.

Some analysts believe that the biotech industry today is where the computer industry was thirty years ago—poised for substantial growth. Currently, there are about 30 commercial products and 700 biotech products in clinical trials.

Of course, there are some major differences between the computer industry and biotechnology. "Their approaches are entirely different from each other," says Nadine Wong, the publisher of the biotech newsletter *BioTech Navigator*. "One is based on machines, the other on humans. Thirty years ago, computers were not available to the public, but look at it now: the PC has become as common as a TV and VCR. Products derived from biotech, on the other hand, are now available to everyone."[5]

If biotechnology lives up to expectations, it could revolutionize modern medicine and, in the process, create significant opportunities for investors. Because of the highly technical nature of the industry, it's difficult to pinpoint the companies and products that will be the first to emerge.

Factors fueling the growth in biotech include:

◆ **Revolutionary approaches.** Traditional pharmaceutical companies develop chemical-based drugs. But, for the most part, these types of drugs only treat the symptoms; they do not cure the disease. The genetic drugs created by biotechnology companies are designed to prevent the cells of a disease from mutating or to kill the cells that are creating the disease.

◆ **Wider applications.** The biotech industry has the brainpower and scope of research to develop cures for such intractable diseases as cancer, heart disease, AIDS, Alzheimer's, and even manic depression. But there are other applications. Biotech may help create alternatives to fossil fuels or help clean the environment by creating microbes that eat radioactive wastes. There are also attempts at creating computer chips out of DNA structures, an initiative that Motorola has been working to perfect.

◆ **Cost-efficiency.** The United States spends $1 trillion each year on health care. Drugs, which are the most cost-efficient means of medical treatment, are allocated 10 percent of that expenditure. And, with emphasis on further cost reductions, drugs are an appealing solution that might receive more focus and increased federal funding in the future.

◆ **Human Genome Project.** In the late 1980s, the U.S. government initiated a program known as the Human Genome Project, with the goal of mapping the complete human genetic code (a process known as *sequencing*). "It will provide a tool for the biotech and pharmaceutical industry to find or develop and even cure disease," says Wong.[6]

Once this massive undertaking is completed, the biotech industry will be poised for fast growth. The government has been spending about $300 million per year on the program since its inception. The Human Genome Project was to be completed by the year 2005. Currently, only about 3 percent of the human genome has been sequenced. Despite this, Wong believes that the project will be completed on time.

FDA APPROVAL

UNDERSTANDING THE FDA approval process is crucial for investing in biotech companies. To sell a drug to the public, the FDA must be convinced that it is safe. Thus, if there is no approval, there is no product and zero revenue. It is primarily for this reason that biotech stocks are so volatile.

Here is a simplified version of the steps a biotech company must take to receive FDA approval:

◆ **Preclinical testing.** When a drug is first developed, the company will conduct preclinical tests (all tests are governed by the FDA, which, unfortunately, leads to long lead times for approval). The drug may be tested on cells of animals to evaluate its safety. If the drug appears to be effective, the company will file an Investigative New Drug (IND) application with the FDA to get approval to test on humans. Success in preclinical testing does not mean the drug is the next Rogaine or Viagra. In fact, many of the drugs that get preclinical approval from the FDA fail when testing is done on humans.

◆ **Phase I: Testing on humans.** This phase typically involves testing on approximately twenty-five paid volunteers. In some cases, these volunteers are prisoners or terminally ill patients. The tests involve variations in dosage in order to determine the safety and side effects of the drug. Phase I testing can take about a month. But, it often stretches to a year because of required FDA paperwork.

◆ **Phase II: Wider testing.** This phase is conducted on a much larger group of people, about 100 to 1,000. It takes months to plan and to set up Phase II, which involves determining the efficacy of the drug based on several different doses. This phase determines how much of the drug can be administered, and also measures the effect on the illness with various doses. The process can last up to two years.

In many ways, this is the most critical phase of the approval process. About 50 percent of the drugs that have success in Phase II ultimately reach the market.

◆ **Phase III: The final phase.** Thousands of people are tested in Phase III, which includes placebo-controlled, "double-blind" tests. That is, one group is given a placebo (which is a sugar pill) and the other is given the drug. "Double-blind" means that neither the patients nor the doctors know who is getting the placebo and who is receiving the real drug. Basically, this test determines if the drug is better than a placebo. The process can last from two to three years.

If the drug is approved at Phase III, the company then files an FDA application for marketing approval. This can take about one year. After this, the company is free to market and sell the drug to the public.

ANALYZING BIOTECH IPOS

ANALYZING BIOTECH IPOs is extremely difficult for most of us. As you read biotech prospectuses, you will notice some highly technical terms, such as *nucleotides, amino acids, monoclonal antibodies,* and *antisense oligonucleotides.* It's almost as though you need to be an M.D. to understand the terminology. In fact, many Wall Street analysts who follow biotech stocks are M.Ds.

Since most biotech IPOs have drugs that are in the development stage, you are essentially analyzing the stock based on the potential outcome of pending research. So, how do you value this research? How can you determine if the company will pass the final phases of FDA approval? It's almost impossible for potential investors to know how a drug will fare in testing. In addition, when a biotech company's drug fails the FDA approval process, the results for the company can be severe.

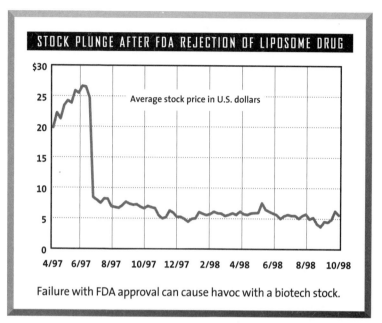

STOCK PLUNGE AFTER FDA REJECTION OF LIPOSOME DRUG

Average stock price in U.S. dollars

Failure with FDA approval can cause havoc with a biotech stock.

For example, in June 1997, Liposome (LIPO) announced that the FDA rejected its drug for respiratory distress syndrome, Ventus. The stock collapsed from $25 to $9.50 in one day.

On the other hand, if the drug receives approval, the rewards can be enormous. Amgen stands out as the prime example. It was able to produce two blockbuster biotech drugs in 1991, Epogen and Neupogen (both now generate $1 billion per year). The company went public in 1983 at $1.50 per share (adjusted for splits). The stock now sells for $70 and has a market capitalization of $14 billion. By any standards, this is phenomenal growth.

Both of these drugs were in the preclinical stage of the approval process when Amgen went public. In fact, it was the release of Epogen and Neupogen that initiated a rush of biotech companies going public in the early 1990s—and the value of most of these companies doubled or tripled. Investors wanted to "get in on the next Amgen." So, Wall Street placated them.

However, then some of the major biotech companies had problems getting approval for their drugs. Some

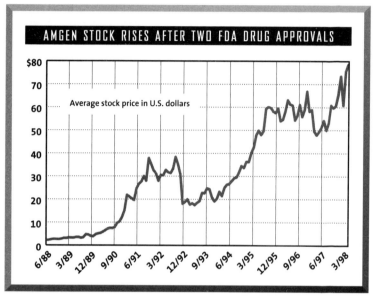

AMGEN STOCK RISES AFTER TWO FDA DRUG APPROVALS

Average stock price in U.S. dollars

were running out of cash. Also, there was talk of major health care reform from Washington. The result was that the market capitalization of biotech companies plunged from $49.3 billion in 1991 to $35 billion three years later.

In general, biotech companies go public at an early stage of corporate development, usually three or four years after being founded. But in the early 1990s, many biotech companies were going public too early—within one or two years of founding. This was definitely too soon, and many investors got burned.

Due to the dicey nature of FDA approval and the difficulty of creating effective drugs, biotech company IPOs have historically been extremely volatile. During the past two years, biotech stocks have fared badly. In 1997, biotech IPOs were down 30 percent, and then an additional 34 percent during the first three quarters of 1998.

This is a sector that requires exceptional stock-picking skills.

DIVERSITY IN THE BIOTECH INDUSTRY

TO MAKE MONEY in biotech, you do not necessarily have to invest in drug-development companies. For example, biotech companies spend approximately $60 billion each year on software, equipment, and services to help build biotech drugs.

Here are businesses that benefit from the biotech revolution:

◆ **Information and research.** Biotech laboratories come in two versions: dry and wet. The wet laboratories are traditional; that is, they have test tubes, microscopes, beakers, and other standard equipment. Dry laboratories involve information; scientists take research and try to find a practical way to use it.

Some of the most enticing investment opportunities evolve in the dry laboratories. One such emerging business is known as bioinformatics, which is the process of managing biotech information. Currently, biotech companies have major problems with information overload (for example, there are 3 billion nucleotides in the human genome). Software solutions will allow for the collaboration of scientists; the proper filtering and storage of information in large relational databases; integration of information sources, such as from the Genome Project; plus gene simulation and prediction tools. Bioinformatics uses software databases to solve the problem of organizing information and making it available in various formats. The fees for such software can be very expensive, which translates into very high margins for these software companies. Incyte charges about $5 million each year for its database software.

◆ **Biotech semiconductors.** Some companies are also developing semiconductor chips (called gene chips) that analyze genetic samples. These chips are specifically designed to process the huge amount of information generated from each DNA strand. The chips will look for patterns in DNA that will help researchers develop new drugs.

◆ **Instruments.** To develop drugs, biotech companies need sophisticated equipment. In fact, the development of this equipment has made great strides in speeding-up the drug development process. Companies that manufacture such equipment are Perseptive Biosystems (PBIO), Biacore International (BCORY), and Molecular Dynamics (MDYN).

◆ **Contract Research Organizations.** These are third-party organizations that help biotech companies recruit patients, design clinical trials, and monitor tests. Parexel (PRXL) and BioReliance (BREL) are both contract research organizations.

STRATEGIES FOR INVESTING IN BIOTECH IPOS

"EVALUATING INITIAL PUBLIC offerings of biotechnology companies, like all IPOs, is subjective," says Wong. "The major problem is the lack of a track record, which makes it difficult to assess the investment and to make a sound decision."[7]

The following is the life cycle of a successful IPO: When the company goes public, the market valuation is typically about $100 million. By the time the company reaches Phase III, it can have a market capitalization of $300 to $500 million. However, if the company gets approval for its drug, the stock is likely to have a market capitalization of well over $1 billion. The reason for this large increase in value is that a biotech company, when it has a product that is selling, has high margins. Companies such as Amgen and Genzyme have margins close to 80 percent.

Before investing in any biotech IPO, take a look at the company's Web site. You're likely to see a wealth of information on the company and perhaps you'll even begin to understand the science. Most importantly, you'll also see what drugs the company has under development and what stages of FDA approval they are in. There is also a Web site detailing FDA clinical trials, called Center Watch (www.CenterWatch.com), which has an abundance of useful information. You can also visit the FDA site at www.fda.gov.com.

These are some factors to look for as you are researching biotech IPOs:

◆ **Experienced management.** As with any IPO, look for a management team with a track record. It is always reassuring if the management has been able to bring a successful drug to market previously. "A company needs to have a balance of business savvy and technical skills,"[8] says Wong.

◆ **Cash position.** "After an IPO, the company should have lots of cash—at least enough to last two years," according to Wong.[9] It takes at least that long to develop a biotech drug and requires a lot of spending.

◆ **Market potential.** Look for companies that have drugs aimed at major markets. For example, cancer treatment is a huge area (it is the second leading cause of death in the United States). Every year, there are 1.4 million new cases of cancer diagnosed and about 70 percent of all cancer patients receive some form of radiation and 50 percent receive chemotherapy, both of which are painful and fraught with side affects. Thus, there is ample room for new and better treatments.

◆ **Pipeline.** Look for companies with a minimum of two drugs under development, at least by Phase II of the process. So, if one drug fails to get approval, the company can focus on the other one.

◆ **Strategic partners.** Look for biotech companies with strong ties to major pharmaceutical companies. First of all, alliances provide biotech companies with much needed capital. Most of these deals involve prepaid royalties on future sales, as well as direct investment. Secondly, alliances allow biotech companies to take advantage of their partner's resources, such as research, employees, and marketing. Finally, the strategic partnership validates the biotech company. In other words, a major pharmaceutical company believes there is potential in the biotech company's technology and is willing to put money and resources into it.

CURRENT AND FUTURE PROSPECTS

ONE EXAMPLE OF A successful biotech IPO is Coulter Pharmaceutical (CLTR). At the time of its IPO, the company was developing a new drug called Bexxar. Its first application is for the treatment of non-Hodgkin's lymphoma (NHL), a cancer of the immune system that afflicts approximately 270,000 people in the United States. So far, the company has been successful at each stage of FDA approval. Coulter is at the forefront of two cutting-edge technologies: conjugated monoclonal antibodies and tumor-activated peptide prodrugs. Not only might both of these help treat cancer, but they might also be effective to treat other diseases. The company went public in January 1997 at an offering price of $12. The current stock price is $24.68.

With the aging of the population around the world and the need to find more cost-effective means for health care, biotech companies are in a position for strong future growth.

To find out more information on biotechnology industry, take a look at these resources:

Biotech Navigator; newsletter written by Scott & Nadine Wong
Sample issue available on the Web at www.biotechnav.com

Medical Technology Stock Letter; newsletter written by James McCamant
Piedmont Venture Group
P.O. Box 40460
Berkeley, CA 94704
510-843-1857

Biotechnology-Health Stock Newsletter; written by Jerry Mullins
601 Penn. Avenue, N.W., Suite 700
Washington, DC 20004
202-508-1475

California Technology Stock Letter; written by Michael Murphy
510-726-8495

CHAPTER

Finance
Sector
IPOs

URING THE LATE 1990s financial stocks soared along with the rising stock market. For example, in January 1997 and July 1998 stocks rose over 40 percent for twenty-one out of fifty-four banks that went public.

But the outlook wasn't always this rosy in the financial sector. During the early 1990s the financial industry was looking rather bleak as bad loans for real estate, leverage buyouts, and credit card delinquencies nearly sank major institutions such as Citicorp and BankofAmerica.

Today, however, there is close to $18 billion in financial sector mutual funds, providing an ongoing demand for finance company IPOs. The finance sector is quite broad, including banking, mutual funds, brokerages, and insurance sectors. Let's take a look at each area and its IPO performance.

BANKING

BANKING HAS BEEN a very hot sector for several years. The momentum in banking is due, in part, to favorable economic trends including:

◆ **A healthy economy.** The U.S. economy has sustained a long period of moderate growth without inflation. This has led to lower delinquencies on bank loans.

◆ **Technology.** New innovations—on-line banking, ATMs, and touch-tone banking—have helped banks cut costs. Automation means more money for the bottom-line.

◆ **Consolidation.** The banking sector has undergone a wave of mergers and acquisitions. This massive consolidation has meant lower costs and higher efficiencies throughout the financial sector. For example, bank mergers mean excess branches can be closed, eliminating duplication.

Some of these finance sector mergers have created impressive powerhouses. The combination of Travelers and Citicorp, a deal worth $80 billion, has operations that serve 100 million customers.

Essentially, these institutions want to build themselves into financial supermarkets that serve all ends of the market with a cornucopia of services and product offerings. This will mean more mergers and acquisitions over the next several years. Even with this merger frenzy, there are still 7,000 banks and 1,000 thrifts in the United States.

◆ **Low interest rates.** Financial companies are intermediaries—they obtain money from depositors by paying them interest. They then take this money and lend it to consumers and businesses at a higher percentage of interest. With low interest rates, banks have been able to obtain money from depositors at a very low rate, thus keeping their costs low. In fact, banking is referred to in jest as the 3-6-3 business: They pay depositors 3 percent, lend money at 6 percent and then tee off at 3 P.M.

As long as the U.S. economy continues to thrive, bank IPOs will be a good sector for investors to target. The best bank IPOs tend to be small companies with strong market niches, which is very enticing to major financial institutions that are looking for merger partners. In fact, if the company does merge with a larger institution, the value of IPO shares is likely to increase.

HOWEVER, WITH THE strong gains in banking stocks during the past few years, it's difficult to find bargains, so you need to be very careful. When investigating bank IPOs, focus on characteristics such as:

◆ **Franchise value.** You want a company that has a dominant position in its market. This is very appealing to big financial institutions that would rather buy an institution instead of building a new market, which is much more costly.

◆ **Fee income.** Financial institutions have been shifting their revenues to fee-based sources—credit cards, mutual funds, insurance, annuities, and asset management. Fee income is desirable because it is less dependent on the pendulum swings in interest rates. A good rule of thumb is to have a financial company with at least 25 percent of its revenues derived from fee-income sources.

Southwest Bancorporation of Texas, Inc. is one example of a successful bank IPO. Regardless of its regional status (it's focused in the Houston area), the company offers products and services that are typically provided by the major banks, such as letters of credit, customized cash management services, brokerage, and mutual funds.

When the company went public, the CEO, Walter E. Johnson, had more than thirty years experience in the banking industry. From 1972 to 1988, he had been president of Allied Bank of Texas, where assets reached $4 billion before it was purchased from First Interstate Bancorp.

When Johnson took control of Southwest Bancorp in 1988, the bank had $43.4 million in assets. By the end of 1996, he had built up $1 billion in assets. For the nine months leading up to September 30, 1996, the company increased its net income by 32.3 percent to $7.4 million. The company went public in January 1997, issuing stock at $8.25 (adjusted for a stock split). The current price is $27.

Anyone looking at the prospectus would have quickly spotted the positive trends: a pattern of increasing net income, a highly experienced management team, and a diverse financial product line.

DESPITE THESE HEALTHY indicators, there are still many risks involved in banking IPOs. Some of the biggest risks include:

◆ **Regional problems.** Small banks can be hit hard by a regional recession. This was a setback for the banks in the farm belt during the 1980s, and for California banks during the real estate collapse of the early 1990s.

◆ **Liberal lending practices.** If a financial institution has a pattern of making bad loans, the impact can be devastating. When the economy is growing as it has been, financial institutions tend to be more liberal with their lending policies. This kind of leveraging is a danger investors should watch for.

MUTUAL FUNDS

MUTUAL FUNDS ARE one of the hottest growth sectors in the financial industry. From 1996 to 1997, investors poured $231 billion into mutual funds.

Much of the growth in this sector can be explained by agreeable demographic trends. The preretirement age group, between the ages of 45 and 64, will grow from 53.7 million in 1996 to 71.1 million in 2005, according to the U.S. Census Bureau. And during the next ten years the baby boom generation is expected to inherit approximately $10 trillion from the previous generation. More money means more investing—and mutual funds are a favorite of baby boomers.

According to Investment Company Institute (ICI), which tracks information for the mutual fund industry, at the end of 1997 there were over 6,800 registered open-end investment companies in the United States.

What many people don't realize is that most mutual funds are private companies with fewer than 100 investment professional employees, yet they are extremely profitable. Furthermore, the mutual fund industry is highly fragmented. This usually means there is great potential for consolidation as bigger mutual funds gobble up smaller ones in an effort to increase market share and reduce costs. There has already been a substantial amount of consolidation: Founders Funds was sold off to Mellon Bank for $275 million in December 1997; Michael Price sold Mutual Shares to Franklin Resources for $800 million in November 1996; and the Clipper Fund was sold to United Asset Management for $125 million in May 1997.

Although this sector continues to have more offerings, mutual fund IPOs have not performed particularly well during the past few years. It is difficult to find specific

RECENT MUTUAL FUND IPOS

◆ **Waddell & Reed Financial Inc.** One of the oldest mutual funds, founded in 1937, the Waddell & Reed in March 1998 had $23.2 billion in assets under management and more than 559,000 customers, holding an average of 2.4 mutual fund accounts per customer. During the past five years, the Waddell & Reed has achieved a 16.8 percent compounded annual growth rate in pretax operating income.

The company did its IPO on March 1998 at $23 per share. The current stock is $22.93.

◆ **Federated Investors.** This is another top-notch mutual fund. The company has been in existence for over forty years and is one of the ten largest mutual funds in the United States, with about $92 billion in assets under management. However, the offering has been lackluster.

The company went public in May 1998 at $19 per share. The stock now trades at $17.87.

explanations. After all, mutual funds have been a fast-growing industry. Perhaps the reason for the bad performance is fear that, if a bear market digs in its claws, mutual funds will suffer greatly as investors pull their money out in droves.

Moreover, it is difficult to find an appropriate valuation for mutual fund IPOs since there are not many similar companies to use as a comparison. It is possible that the recent mutual fund IPOs were priced at high valuations. Finally, many of the recent mutual fund IPOs were offered during a period when the IPO market was showing lackluster performance, which may have put pressure on the stocks.

Given such performances, it is not easy to find a formula spotting solid mutual fund IPOs. However, here are some commonsense guidelines.

◆ **Investing in portfolio managers.** Peter Lynch's tremendous success with the Magellan fund catapulted Fidelity into the stratosphere as it became the biggest mutual fund company in the world. This is an extreme example, but the principle holds up. Look for a mutual fund IPO that has strong portfolio managers with consistently positive long-term performance records.

◆ **Technology.** Look for mutual funds that are spending money on information systems that help the portfolio managers make better decisions.

◆ **Growth.** Look for growth in earnings and assets under management. The more money a mutual fund manages, the better, because compensation is based on a percentage of the assets under management (1 percent to 3 percent).

◆ **Marketing.** A mutual fund needs to spend money on sales and marketing to increase assets under management. With thousands of mutual funds competing, sales and marketing are crucial to success.

BROKERAGES

DISCOUNT BROKERAGE FIRMS were introduced in 1975. Before then, brokerage commissions were fixed. But when Congress deregulated commission rates, it sowed the seeds of today's financial revolution. Firms like Schwab and Quick & Reilly were first to offer customers low commission rates, which lead to much higher trading volumes.

As a result of these reduced fees and increased accessibility to the financial markets, more people are becoming comfortable handling their own investments. They do their own research, set their investment goals, and invest on their own time. During the past few years, several on-line brokerage firms have gone public and have done quite well.

One of the reasons for this success is market consolidation. Many of the major financial institutions have been purchasing brokerage firms at very high valuations. This is likely to continue, as there are fewer and fewer independent brokerage firms. This consolidation helps to cut costs and to boost the industry.

The do-it-yourself investment trend is another significant factor that has contributed to the huge success of the on-line brokers. There are about 3 million on-line accounts at the time of this writing. True, this represents a relatively small amount of the total 80 million brokerage accounts. But, according to a study by Forrester Research, by the year 2002, there are expected to be 14 million on-line accounts with $700 billion in assets.

Brokerage stocks and IPOs include some major risks:

◆ **Market volatility.** A decrease in trading volume would result in reduced transaction revenues and a decrease in profitability for brokerage firms. When times are good, these stocks do very well; in bad times, they suffer. Brokerages are trying to diversify out of the commission business. E*Trade, for example, offers mortgages on its Web site.

◆ **Price competition.** Increased technology and thickening competition have generated tremendous pressure to decrease prices and, thus, commission rates. For example, E*Trade cut its commission seven times during the past four years. So far, increases in trading volume have offset reduced commissions, but this momentum in volume can't continue forever.

◆ **Liability.** On-line brokerages are subject to power failures and technological mishaps. This happened to E*Trade and other on-line brokerages during October 27 and 28, 1997, resulting in a sticky PR situation. And, what if an on-line brokerage firm is down for, say, a week?

Factors indicating strong IPOs in this sector include:

◆ **Effective marketing.** Schwab, for example, has been in existence since the mid-1970s and over time has built an incredible brand name by doing smart marketing. Since the on-line brokerage market is very competitive, upstart companies must gain the attention and trust of investors.

E*Trade (EGRP) held its successful brokerage IPO in August 1996. As a pioneer in the on-line brokerage category, it was one of the first to allow customers to trade over the Internet, beginning in February 1996. As a result, the company has established a valuable brand name.

At the time of the IPO, E*Trade had over 73,000 accounts, with an average monthly growth rate of 11 percent. Its average daily trading volume was 8,000, compared to 4,200 only a year earlier.

The IPO prospectus mentions that a main goal of E*Trade was to engage in aggressive marketing by opening more and more accounts (in the past two years, E*Trade has spent $38 million on marketing). So far, it has been a very successful strategy. By 1998, the company reported $104.4 million in revenues for the first six months of fiscal 1998, up 83 percent from the prior year. Net income during this period soared 108 percent to $11 million. In all, E*Trade had over 400,000 accounts and assets exceeded $10 billion.

◆ **Reliance on non-price factors.** To avoid price wars, on-line brokers are finding value-added services to offer. For example, E*Trade offers its users mortgages on-line, and has also purchased a company, called ShareData, to provide customers with sophisticated stock option services.

◆ **Distribution agreements.** On-line brokerages want customers, customers, and more customers. Because fees are low, achieving a critical mass customer base is necessary for success. On-line brokerages have spent millions to get exclusive placements on high traffic sites like AOL, Yahoo!, or Excite!. However, these arrangements shut out other on-line brokers, making it more difficult for them to compete. In other words, the newer on-line brokers will have a much tougher time than the current majors—Ameritrade, E*Trade, Schwab—that have a large head start.

◆ **Web features.** Another way on-line brokerages set themselves apart is by offering so-called technological "bells and whistles." E*Trade has an area for on-line chat, as well as cool Java charting of stocks.

INSURANCE

ONE OF THE keys to the success of Warren Buffett was entry into the insurance industry. He saw the great potential of the industry. People paid money on a consistent basis for protection from problems of health, disability, and unexpected death. However, the payment of claims was many years in the future, so Buffett was able to use the large amounts of incoming cash to invest in the bond and stock markets.

The insurance company, in this scenario, is really an investment company. If the portfolio managers are talented and the company does not take excessive risks, the profits can be substantial.

Insurance companies that choose to go public are usually large organizations. It is not uncommon for an insurance company IPO to raise more than $100 million in capital. In May 1997, the Hartford Life IPO raised $650 million.

When perusing the IPO prospectus of an insurance firm, look for factors that point to:

◆ **Brand name.** Look for an insurance company that has strong customer loyalty and brand recognition. For the

INSURANCE COMPANY IPOS

◆ **Hartford Life.** The company has a broad product line—with annuities, retirement plans, life insurance, employee benefits, disability insurance, and so on. It has seen its assets grow from $23 billion in 1992 to $80 billion in 1996. Since the IPO in February 1997, the stock price has increased by 107 percent.

◆ **Nationwide Financial Services.** The company administers about 15,000 pension plans. From 1992 to 1996, Nationwide's assets grew from $20.8 billion to $47.8 billion. The company launched its IPO in March 1997; since then the stock has increased by 115 percent.

most part, insurance is a commodity business, and the difference between one type of life insurance policy is not much different from that of another company. Often, the biggest difference is the price of the policy. To compete in this environment, insurance companies must have a strong brand name in order to attract new customers—without having to reduce prices and, thus, margins.

◆ **Reserves.** Look at the risk factors in the prospectus and see if the insurance company has sufficient reserves. Focus on those companies that have a high credit rating (such as AAA from Moody's). There have been cases of top-rated insurance companies failing, but such a failure is rare.

◆ **Asset base.** Look for strong growth compared to the industry in terms of assets under management. A large part of an insurance company's compensation is based on how much money it manages.

◆ **Cost cutting.** Look for an efficient organization. Are the administrative costs rising faster than the revenues? If so, such unbalanced spending will hurt profitability and the stock price.

CONCLUSION

THE FINANCIAL INDUSTRY is diverse. Investors should weigh the advantages and disadvantages of each sector and realize that these segments of the industry do not behave exactly alike. However, with the growth of U.S. investments, the prospects for finance company IPOs look bright as long as the stock market doesn't take a major tumble.

CHAPTER

10

Retail Sector IPOs

OME OF THE greatest IPO fortunes have been made from retail companies such Wal-Mart, Home Depot, and Starbucks. The main reason is *scalability,* the ability to sell large quantities in many geographic markets. That is, once you have the blueprint for one store, it is easy to duplicate it across the United States and the world.

But finding the right blueprint can be difficult. The retail industry is rife with competition and reels from the rapid changes in consumer tastes. For example, of the thirty-six retail companies that went public between 1997 and 1998 (as of August), twenty-four were below their offering price.

So, to be successful with retail company IPOs, you need to do your homework and have some luck, too. Here are the factors to look for in your analysis:

◆ **Big market.** Sift for retailers that are in markets that have long-term growth potential. An example is the drugstore industry. With an aging population and increased reliance on prescription medication, drugstore IPOs have done very well in recent years.

◆ **Value/quality.** Wal-Mart founder Sam Walton revolutionized the retailing industry. In his stores, he provided customers with quality products, tremendous selection, and low prices.

Two recent retail IPOs illustrate this approach well. Duane Reade, for example, is a New York City drugstore chain that provides impressive selection, quality products, and prices that average 10 percent lower than competitors. It went public in February 1998 at $16.50; today shares are $38. CD Warehouse also follows a similar recipe with its pre-owned compact discs. CDs last a long time with no sacrifice of sound quality. The company's motto is "selling compact discs at compact prices." CD Warehouse went public January 1997 at $5; today it's trading at $18.

◆ **Fragmented industry with M&A potential.** Look for those retail companies that are in disfranchised markets. This makes it easier for an IPO company to grow since it can purchase smaller retail operations, usually at bargain prices. For example, a key element to the growth of Blockbuster Video was in acquiring smaller video chains. Within a decade, Blockbuster Video was the largest video chain in the nation.

However, to succeed in a fragmented industry, the management of a company needs experience in mergers and acquisitions. Thus, look for those retail company IPOs that have already successfully merged in the past few years.

◆ **Favorable industry statistics.** A common statistic is "sales per square foot." Basically, this indicates the efficiency of a store. For example, Duane Reade led the drugstore industry with a sales per square feet of $956. This was two times the national average.

Also, look at a company's same store sales compared to competitors. Same store sales show the growth of those stores that have been in existence for at least one year.

◆ **Brand recognition.** When you hear the word "McDonald's," you instantly know what to expect: Big Macs, fries.

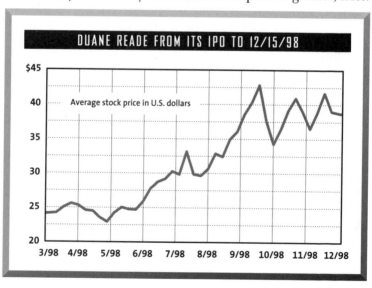

DUANE READE FROM ITS IPO TO 12/15/98

Average stock price in U.S. dollars

Powerful branding enhances a company's competitive situation. Starbucks, for example, has become the biggest retailer of coffee by establishing an incredible brand name. It managed to set itself apart first and then stay ahead of the hundreds of other specialty coffee stores that that popped up to imitate its success.

SUCCESSFUL RETAIL IPOS

◆ **Duane Reade.** This is the largest drugstore chain in New York City. Fifty-eight of its sixty-seven stores are in the high-traffic areas of Manhattan. The company had a long history of posting strong revenue and earnings gains. Operating profits increased from $26.9 million (for the fifty-two weeks ended March 29, 1996) to $41.2 million (for the fifty-two weeks ended September 27, 1997). The company completed its IPO in February 1998. The offering price was $16.50; the stock currently trades at $38.

◆ **Horizon Pharmacies Inc.** Like Duane Reade, Horizon is a pharmacy that emphasizes wide selection, customer service, and low prices. It has fourteen retail stores and was named as one of the top pharmacies in the country by *Chain Drug Review*. Horizon has been growing fast. From 1995 to 1996, sales increased from $6.8 million to $13.1 million. The company did its IPO in July 1997 at $5 per share. The stock is now selling for $10.

◆ **Sonic Automotive.** This company has twenty auto dealerships in addition to four used vehicle facilities and eight collision repair centers. It has a great management team. The founder and CEO, O. Bruton Smith, has over thirty years of automotive retailing experience, and the other executives have, on average, eighteen years of experience. What's more, the company's dealerships have won a variety of awards for quality and excellence. The company completed its IPO in November 1997 at $12 per share. The stock is now selling for $28.

BEFORE BUYING A retail company IPO, you should know
to look for certain danger signs. Steer clear of companies
that have problems such as:

◆ **Fad appeal.** Certain retail areas, such as toys and cloth-
ing stores, are apt to fall victim to volatile earnings as a
result of fads. When the fad is alive, the sales and profits
can be enormous. But, of course, when it ends, sales and
profits will collapse. For more information on fads, read
Chapter 15.

◆ **Regional concentration.** It is common for retailers to
have operations focused in a certain area of the country.
The problem here is that if there is a downturn in the
local economy, the company can be severely affected.
It's better to focus on retailers that have at least some
regional diversification. A business such as McDonald's,
that has stores all around the globe, is safer because it
has many regional markets to rely on.

Many retailers use the capital earned from an IPO to
expand their markets. If a company you are looking at has
a narrow geographical focus, check the IPO prospectus for
diversification plans.

◆ **Weak franchising.** Franchising can be a tremendous way
to increase the size of a retail operation. This is what
turned McDonald's and Burger King into fast food powerhouses. CD Warehouse, too, is based on the franchise
model and was named in *Entrepreneur Magazine*'s top
thirty new franchises in the United States in 1997.

But there are risks to the franchising model. Quality is
not universally upheld store to store because it is difficult
to control the actions of a franchise's owner. Consistency
can be a real problem. For example, many food franchises
fail to provide quality service and, in general, uphold the
standards of a well-run restaurant. And some franchise-
based retailers have engaged in accounting shenanigans.
Boston Market, for example, was a hot IPO in 1995, rising
from $15 to $36. Unfortunately, it accounted for its franchise fees in an inappropriate manner and the stock is now
trading at only $1.

CONCLUSION

IF THERE'S ONE great piece of advice to follow before investing in a retail IPO, it's this: Visit the retail store. See with your own eyes how business is doing. Is the store clean? Is the service good? How about the prices?

True, this is a subjective approach—but great investors, Peter Lynch included, have made a lot of money using this simple strategy. You can, too.

CHAPTER

11

Foreign
IPOs

O OTHER COUNTRY has as many IPOs each year as the United States. In fact, when foreign companies plan IPOs, they often seek advice from U.S. investment banks.

The U.S. stock market, however, accounts for only one-third of all equity in the world, so someone focusing exclusively on investments in the United States is missing most of the opportunities. The returns in foreign markets can be breathtaking. For example, the Turkish stock market soared an unbelievable 634 percent between January 1989 and July 1990.

International investing can also add diversification to your portfolio, because foreign markets are not always in sync with market cycles in the United States. When the U.S. market is down, a variety of foreign markets will be up. And many nations right now are growing more quickly than the United States. The stocks in these nations, too, sometimes sell at very low valuations, compared to historically high valuations in America.

Successful IPOs in any market depend upon growth, and foreign markets, overall, have a lot of room for growth in many emerging market sectors.

TRENDS IN FOREIGN MARKETS

INVESTING IN FOREIGN markets gives an investor the chance to find the next AT&T or McCaw Cellular. For example, there are fewer than 7 phone lines per 100 people in Brazil compared to 60 per 100 people in the United States. But when the Brazilian tele-communications industry is fully privatized, this situation could change rapidly and present a potentially hot opportunity for investors.

The major phone company in Brazil is Telebras, which was listed on the NYSE Exchange in late 1997. Since then, the stock has soared. Despite this, the stock still sells at a PE ratio of about 11—relatively low compared to U.S. telecom stocks, such as WorldCom, which can trade at PE ratios over 50.

Many foreign nations have been and will continue privatizing their main industries. And IPOs are at the very center of this process, because issuing stock to the public facilitates privatization. When a company goes from being a nationalized business to a private one, there is a lot of immediate potential for IPO growth. Here are some factors that explain why privatization and other developments in foreign nations create opportunities for investors:

◆ **Privatization.** When a government owns a business, the motives of the company are more political than economic, resulting many times in poor management. But once a company is privatized, it is free to compete and to innovate. Privatization can lead to higher profitability through reduced cost structure, and it provides incentives for managers and employees to have a greater stake in the company's success.

◆ **Proliferation of free markets.** For many years after World War II, many countries were governed by communist regimes. Communism prevented the creation of a fertile market for enterprise as we know it. After the fall of the Berlin Wall, a great many countries moved in the direction of capitalism and democracy. This means that there will be many more IPOs for state-owned businesses. Investors will be able to purchase telephone companies, oil companies, water utilities, and other major infrastructure companies that have huge potential

◆ **Education.** The literacy rates in many countries have been soaring, increasing industry capabilities. Productive work forces are already apparent in Asian markets such as Hong Kong, South Korea, and Singapore, countries with strict educational imperatives. Until the recent slowdown in Asia, these countries experienced tremendous growth. Employees able to maximize innovation and technology create new businesses, unleashing entrepreneurial activity, which speeds growth, and translates into increased stock values.

◆ **Technology.** The adoption of PCs, faxes, the Internet, and other modern technology has had a tremendous impact on the growth rates of many foreign nations. Ironically, many foreign countries have the advantage of seeing what has worked in the developed nations. Many emerging foreign countries are using digital and cellular communications instead of analogue technologies, because they are more cost-effective and offer better quality and features. With a state-of-the art technology infrastructure, companies grow more easily and more quickly.

◆ **Less protectionism.** Many foreign countries recognize that free trade is vitally important to strong economic growth and have been reducing tariffs, eliminating currency restrictions, and making it easier for foreigners to invest in the stock market. A major example is Argentina, which has undergone radical free-market policies. The result has been tremendous economic growth and strong stock values.

◆ **Demographics.** Many foreign countries are enjoying great improvements in health care, lengthening life spans, and lower infant mortality rates. As a rule, a healthier population means that people have more time to devote to economic activity, instead of trying merely to survive.

◆ **Savings.** It is typical for smaller nations to have a high savings rate. The major reason is that there usually is not much for consumers to buy. Additionally, people in poverty tend to be very thrifty.

A high savings rate is fuel for fast economic growth. For example, Singapore has a savings rate that represents 47 percent of gross domestic product (GDP). These savings are invested in new ventures via the IPO market, as well as in existing stocks. With more and more companies going into these stocks, the values increase.

HOW TO INVEST
IN FOREIGN MARKETS

ADRS ARE THE best, easiest way for U.S. consumers to invest in foreign markets.

An American Depository Receipt (ADR) is a foreign company that is actually listed on a U.S. stock exchange, making it much easier to get price quotes—even for IPO shares. Furthermore, ADRs do not require dealing with an overseas broker; rather, a U.S. full-service or discount broker can handle trades.

Technically, ADRs are not really stocks. Here's why: Suppose you want to buy 100 shares of the "XYZ" ADR. It is listed on the New York Stock Exchange and trades at $10 per share. You would call your broker, who would phone another broker in Hong Kong, who would purchase the shares. The foreign broker will then deposit these shares in a U.S. bank, and the bank will issue a certificate, called an *ADR*, to your local broker.

When you decide to sell, you will call your broker, who will call the Hong Kong broker. This broker will sell the shares and you receive your money.

Even though you will receive your money in U.S. dollars, there is currency risk involved in buying ADRs. In fact, the foreign broker is actually exchanging U.S. dollars with foreign currency. This is why there is often a price difference between ADRs and the real stock as it's listed on the foreign exchange.

The other option is to buy directly from a foreign exchange or broker. This preference is definitely for brave souls. You will be paying high commissions. You will need to deal with the headaches of archaic market systems, and you most likely will be required to have a high minimum investment level. Buying direct is more suited for market professionals.

RISKS

IN ADDITION TO opportunities, there are also major risks associated with investing in foreign companies.

◆ **Risk of political strife.** Developing nations are susceptible to wrenching political chaos, which inevitably harms stock prices. Mexico is a prime example: In 1994 there was a violent peasant revolt in Chiapas. Presidential candidate Luis Donaldo Colosio Murrieta, who was to succeed the current President, was assassinated. The discord caused investors to pull their money out of the country and the stock market collapsed.

But political risk is not limited to riots or assassinations. Perhaps the more common type of political risk is the influence of government policy, such as, heavy taxes, a lax monetary policy, or harsh trade restrictions.

However, the most serious threat to investors is when a foreign government "nationalizes" business. When a government takes over a private business, investors lose everything.

◆ **Risk of default.** A default on government debts can have a devastating impact on stock prices. During the 1980s investors pulled money out of third world nation stocks when defaults lowered confidence in the economic stability of those countries.

◆ **Currency risk.** Another factor in the fall of Mexico's stock market was the devaluation of the peso. As discussed above, buying foreign stocks involves currency risk, whether you are utilizing ADRs or buying stock directly. There are financial techniques to reduce the currency risk, called *hedging*. However, hedging is too expensive for individual investors, more suitable for institutional investors.

◆ **Market risk.** Every market moves between bull and bear modes—this is normal. However, some countries will attempt to intervene to prevent market forces. For example, in 1983, the Israeli stock market collapsed and the government, as a result, suspended trading for two weeks. Such an action means you have no liquidity. If you need to sell your stock (to buy a car or pay for your education), you are out of luck until the markets reopen. In fact, when a government closes a stock market, investors know there are serious problems; so when the markets reopen it is common for the plunge to continue.

The U.S. market is not immune from having its markets closed. This happened in October 1997 when the markets closed for several hours because of heavy volatility. However, this closure was meant to give investors time to cool off. In this case, it worked out and the market rebounded.

♦ **Information risk.** It is difficult for individuals to find timely information on foreign economies, because the information may be in another language and obtaining it is expensive (although, the Internet is starting to change this).

The U.S. securities markets have the most thorough laws for disclosure of information, but disclosure requirements in the foreign markets tend to be very lax, almost nonexistent. Different accounting systems and standards, too, can make analysis confusing, and many of these countries do not have many stock analysts. But remember, the lack of information can be a benefit in some cases, because there is a higher chance of inefficiency in the pricing of the stocks from which a wise investor can profit.

♦ **Custody risk.** Many foreign markets have antiquated payment systems. It can take several weeks to sell your stocks or even receive your certificates. In Russia, for example, stock purchases are registered by hand. Since

WARNING

BE CAREFUL: Foreign IPOs purchased by U.S. citizens must be registered with the Securities and Exchange Commission. Click on the "EDGAR Database" button on the SEC's Web site (www.sec.gov) to confirm that the IPO is listed (see p. 57).

clears are written on paper (there are no computers), it is easy to manipulate trades. In fact, there are examples of companies that have forged stock certificates and bilked investors.

INVESTING TIPS

BEFORE YOU START to invest in foreign markets, it's a good idea to be comfortable first investing in the United States and to build a level of sophistication and understanding of the investment process.

Here are some other tips for investors who are ready to send their money abroad:

◆ **Stick with what you know.** As with almost any type of investing, your best bet is to invest in an area that you are familiar with. If you travel frequently and have a strong understanding of the investment climate and upcoming business developments in a specific region, then this is a good region to start with.

◆ **Invest for the long-term.** Currency fluctuations can wreak havoc on your foreign investments in the short-term. However, over the long-term, the volatility tends to be reduced. Also, frequent buying and selling of foreign stocks can be very expensive since the commissions are high and the liquidity low.

◆ **Understand cross-border accounting.** Suppose you see that a foreign stock is selling at a PE ratio of 4. Sounds cheap, right? The stock may actually be expensive, because the country might have different accounting standards from the United States. In 1992, when Brilliance China Automotive Company went public on the New York Stock Exchange, auditors spent 11,000 hours to restate the financial data.

◆ **Be wary of economic statistics.** In a myriad of foreign nations, there is a thriving underground economy, also known as the *black market.* Countries may have stiff laws against certain economic transactions, or may not allow charging interest on loans. Despite this, private citizens take their activities underground. In many cases, the gov-

SPECIAL ADVICE ON FOREIGN STOCK

◆ **Try Schwab.** Many discount brokers do not have the resources to provide for investment in foreign stocks. The one exception is Charles Schwab, which has spent a lot of money developing its international trading desk.

◆ **Aftermarket support.** The U.S. market has the most advanced financial distribution centers in the world. In a week, its financial system can handle billions in IPOs, although the same is not true in other countries. There is a greater likelihood that, over time, foreign IPOs will fall in price. The reason is that these countries do not have many financial institutions to help support the stocks.

◆ **Research on the Web.** The Web is a global medium and a cost-effective method for researching foreign companies. The best way to get the information you need is to visit a foreign stock exchange's Web site. The Helsinki Stock Exchange page (www.hse.fi) provides access to twenty-two of the seventy-two companies listed (such as Web addresses, e-mail, English press releases, and so on). A variety of emerging market stock exchanges are listed, such as the one in Chile, which has information on twenty-three ADRs.

Here are some stock exchanges you may want to visit:

ISTANBUL (www.ise.org)

SANTIAGO (www.bolsantiago.cl)

TOKYO (www.tse.org)

SEOUL (www.kse.or.kr)

You can also find useful information from the Web pages of global investment banks, such as CS First Boston (www.csfirstboston.com) and Morgan Stanley (www.morgan.com).

ernment statistics do not account for the activities, which results in faulty economic statistics.

◆ **Steer clear of conflicts of interest.** The laws regarding the duties of senior managers and even brokers in some nations can be lax. For example, some countries allow companies to engage in activities that benefit the senior managers at the expense of shareholders—which is often the case with family-controlled companies (these families may even be part of a royal family). Some countries also allow brokers to buy on their account before they make a purchase for their client, known as *front-running*. And, of course, political corruption can have a profound effect on a country's markets. In 1996, Korea's head securities regulator was arrested for taking bribes from companies seeking approval for listing on the country's exchange.

So, before you purchase a foreign IPO, you need to do some homework. It will often take you longer to do the research compared to the amount you would do for a U.S. IPO, but it is worth the effort.

CONCLUSION

BECAUSE OF THE difficulty involved with investing in foreign markets, individual investors should consider mutual funds that specialize in overseas companies instead of picking stocks individually. There are no mutual funds that specialize solely in foreign IPOs, but many funds that specialize in global stocks participate in IPOs and have done quite well in the process.

OTHER IPO
Investments

IPO Mutual
FUNDS

WITH OVER 8,000 mutual funds on the market, it seems only natural that some would invest heavily in IPOs—and there are several that do. After all, as stated in the Introduction, mutual funds buy a large percentage of all IPO shares. Until now, this has been a well-kept secret.

Mutual funds do not like to announce that they invest in IPOs, because IPOs are risky. But, with the recent surge in IPOs, this attitude is changing fast. Renaissance Capital, founded in 1991, is not afraid to advertise an IPO connection. In 1998 it launched the IPO Plus Aftermarket Fund (also called IPO Fund).

The fund is still very new, so it is not appropriate to make comparisons (at least two years' statistics would be necessary), but as of December 1998, the fund was up 4 percent. However, this is still relatively strong, considering that the market went into a tailspin during this period.

According to its charter, the IPO Fund has the objective of investing at least 65 percent of its assets in IPOs at the time of the offering and in the aftermarket (which, according to academics, is considered to be up to ten years after the offering). What's more, the portfolio managers are allowed to invest up to 25 percent of the assets in foreign IPOs. Finally, up to 15 percent of the assets can be invested in illiquid investments (these are investments that cannot be sold within seven days).

The IPO Fund does not focus solely on small companies or high-tech IPOs, but portfolio manager Linda R. Killian claims, "Our portfolio is a reflection of what is happening in the IPO market. If a lot of technology companies are going public during any one period, investors can be assured that the IPO Fund will have a high proportion of tech stocks in it."[10]

However, the fund looks for quality deals. As with any mutual fund, its aim is to make money: "We focus only on IPOs that have market capitalizations of more than $50 million," says Killian. "Anything less than that is usually not a quality deal. We analyze IPOs according to four criteria: fundamentals, management control issues (e.g., does management own stock?), the trading momentum in similar companies, and the valuation," continues Killian. "We always attend the road shows and often meet with management privately at 'one on ones.' We also dig into the company's relative position in the industry by calling competitors."[11]

A team of portfolio managers runs the fund: Killian focuses on retailers, health care, and telecom; Kathleen Smith covers technology, and her husband William Smith researches leverage buyouts (LBOs) and capital goods companies.

Although there are a variety of mutual funds that invest in IPOs, the IPO Fund is the one with the most focused investment objective.

ADVANTAGES OF IPO MUTUAL FUNDS

THERE ARE MANY reasons for individual investors to choose IPO mutual funds instead of picking their own IPO stocks:

◆ **Diversification.** For a minimum investment you can get instant diversification. A portfolio manager has the capital to purchase many IPOs at once. So, if one falls in value, it is likely that some of the others will increase in value. This what diversification is all about; it helps reduce volatility. IPO Fund chooses between twenty and forty companies for its portfolio; other similar funds would do the same. To manage this level of diversification yourself would be quite costly.

◆ **Professional management.** Portfolio managers have education and investment experience that individual investors simply do not. They also have a staff to help with the leg work. IPO Fund, for example, has been doing IPO research for nine years. Its research database includes proprietary information on 2,000 IPOs. Investors of the fund get the benefit of this research.

◆ **Clout and contacts.** Because of the large amount of money they have under management, the IPO Fund and other mutual funds have the advantage of obtaining hot IPOs at the offering price. Portfolio managers also have contacts, attend conferences, and talk to management. In many cases, they will know about events before they are reported to the public. They may know which IPOs will be hot and which are rumored to collapse.

◆ **Convenience.** You can buy mutual funds over the phone, or by mail, and even over the Internet. Investing in IPOs directly is a bit more difficult and time consuming, so you might also consider calling a broker, insurance company, or bank.

NO FREE LUNCH

MUTUAL FUNDS THAT specialize in IPOs tend to have comparatively high fees. Here are some of the different types of fees:

◆ **Loads.** This is a commission to the broker who sells you the fund. Some loads are charged when you buy the fund. For example, if you put $1,000 into a mutual fund and it has a 4 percent load, you will pay $40 in commission. So, in order to break even, your fund will have to increase by 4.16 percent. There are also back-end loads, which are charged when you sell the fund. The longer you hold the fund, the less the commission is.

◆ **12b-1 fee.** This is also known as a *distribution* or *marketing fee*. It is a sales commission that is deducted every year you hold the fund. The maximum that can be charged is 1 percent of your investment.

◆ **Management fee.** Even if you buy a no-load fund, you still need to pay this fee. It covers research expenses, such as purchasing subscriptions to investment services and salaries for portfolio managers.

MUTUAL FUND STRATEGIES

HERE ARE SOME tips for investing in mutual funds that have a large exposure to IPOs:

◆ **Use dollar-cost averaging.** Many mutual funds have systematic investment programs: you can have the fund automatically deduct a certain amount, say, $100 or $1,000 or more, from your bank account each month or each quarter. This way, you will not be exposing all of your funds at once, but will instead be gradually and steadily investing your money. This strategy is called *dollar-cost-averaging.* When the shares are selling at a low price, you will be buying a lot, but when the shares are high, you will be buying less. In effect, you are buying low. This is a good strategy for investing in IPOs, since there is a high degree of volatility and the market is difficult to predict.

Reinvesting capital gains and dividends is another great way to use dollar-cost averaging: Most funds allow such reinvestment. But keep in mind: Even if you put the capital gains and dividends back into the fund, you are still taxed on them.

◆ **Read the prospectus.** Just as every IPO has a prospectus, so does every mutual fund. Both documents are similar. You'll see information on past performance, the management team, fees, and the fund's objective.

◆ **Ask for help.** Most mutual funds have an 800 number. You should use it whenever you need information on the fund, an explanation of fund performance, or even industry trends. Also, ask how much of the fund's assets are invested in IPOs. Get the most out of those fees.

◆ **Read the proxy statements.** A mutual fund must get shareholder consent to make any major policy changes. This is done via a *proxy,* a document sent to shareholders. Read these documents and vote; it can make a difference. Perhaps the biggest thing to look for is a change in the objective of the fund. For example, suppose you invest in an IPO mutual fund that has the objective to invest 80 percent of its funds in IPOs and suddenly wants to lower this to 50 percent. These are things that investors should know. You should also pay close attention to changes in fees.

◆ **Correctly monitor performance.** Compare your fund to others like it. For the most part, IPO funds are microcap funds. So, it makes sense to weigh your IPO fund against other such microcap funds instead of the S&P 500, which has larger, more established companies, and would not provide an accurate comparison.

◆ **Know your fund manager.** You are not just investing in the fund, but in one or more portfolio managers. These people decide what to buy and sell. If a respected, successful portfolio manager leaves the fund, then you may want to leave, too, unless the new manager has an investment philosophy you believe in.

◆ **Know the fund's holdings.** You can request information from the mutual fund that shows the top holdings. What types of companies does the fund own? Are IPOs in the top holdings? If so, are they the type of companies you feel comfortable investing in?

IPO FUNDS

MORE ON THE IPO FUND

THE IPO FUND has a relatively low minimum investment of $2,500. If you want to start an IRA, the minimum is $500, plus a subsequent $100 per month. There are no front or back-end sales fees, but it does have a 0.25 percent trailing commission per year. The total expenses are 2.5 percent, which is somewhat high for a mutual fund. The fund also has a high (200 percent) turnover rate. That is, the fund will hold onto a stock for, on average, only one quarter. In other words, the fund takes a very short-term approach to investing.

"The nature of IPO investing is rapid turnover," says Killian. "When the IPO calendar is strong, we may sell stocks of companies that have achieved our price targets to free up funds for upcoming IPOs. Stocks of IPOs also tend to be volatile, due to the small capitalization nature of many of them, unseasoned trading, and lack of independent

research. So, as portfolio managers we have to be respon-
sive to the volatile trading in these stocks and take profits
when opportunity presents."[12]

This is not to imply that the fund does not invest for the
long term. According to Killian, the two biggest positions
in her fund are Keebler and Equant, both of which she
intends to hold for the long term. "These are companies
that have solid track records and are leaders in the
fields,"[13] says Killian.

But high turnover can have significant costs. First of all,
the fund will incur relatively high transaction costs (i.e.,
commissions). Second, if the fund sells many of its holdings at a profit, these will be classified as capital gains, which
will be passed directly to the shareholders. The reason is
that mutual funds are not taxed, the investors are. Therefore, Killian believes that her fund is best suited for non-
taxable accounts, such as IRAs, Keoghs, and Roth IRAs.

KAUFMAN FUND

THE MANAGERS OF the Kaufman Fund, Lawrence Auriana
and Hans Utsch (both of whom have over thirty years of
Wall Street experience), are top-notch money managers.
They invest in a variety of industries, such as technology,
health care, and retailing, and they look for small market
capitalizations between $50 million to $1 billion.

This duo's investment philosophy is based on scouting
for companies with proprietary products targeted at multi-
billion-dollar industries, class A managements, and strong
profit histories of at least 20 percent per year. In fact,
before buying a company, Auriana and Utsch will interview
the management team and its suppliers and customers.

IPOs comprise 30 to 40 percent of the portfolio. The
Kaufman fund has a hefty expense ratio of 1.89 percent.
The minimum initial investment is $1,500 and $500 for
retirement accounts. During the past ten years, the fund
has returned 18.11 percent per year. However, in the past
five years, the fund returned 12.5 percent per year, which
underperformed the S&P by 6 percent per year.

MUNDER MICROCAP EQUITY FUND

THIS FUND HAS a modest $6 million under management. However, more than 50 percent of these assets are invested in IPOs. Munder Microcap focuses on companies with strong earnings potential, superior technology, exceptional management, and market capitalizations below $200 million. The minimum investment is $250 and the expense ratio is 1.5 percent.

The fund is been in existence only since 1997, in which it returned 71 percent. However, as of September 1998, the fund was down 27 percent (which was actually 1 percent better than the S&P). The reason for the fall was the large correction in the stock market during September.

ROBERTSON STEPHENS MICROCAP GROWTH

THIS FUND INVESTS in companies with market capitalizations of $250 million or less. Dave Evans, the portfolio manager, looks for stocks that are underfollowed, underowned, and undervalued, and many in the IPO sector are. Besides looking for revenue and earnings growth of 20+ percent per year, Evans does extensive interviews with management.

The fund averages about half of its portfolio in IPOs, has an expense ratio of 1.95 percent, and has about $100 million in assets. The minimum investment is $5,000 and $1,000 for retirement accounts.

OPPENHEIMER ENTERPRISE

THIS FUND HAS about $130 million in assets and seeks out undiscovered investment opportunities, particularly from the IPO market. Jay Tracey, the portfolio manager, looks for companies with market capitalizations of $200 million or less. The fund invests about half its assets in IPOs, and the minimum investment is $1,000 with an expense ratio of 0.91 percent.

Check out the Resources section on page 238 for contact information on the funds listed in this chapter.

13

Virtual
IPOs

ECHNOLOGY HAS BEEN a driving force in financial markets. It's hard to believe, but Nasdaq, the computerized trading system that handles over one billion shares, did not even exist thirty years ago. There was no computer system that could handle so many transactions. Stocks and bonds had to be traded on a physical trading floor, such as the New York Stock Exchange (NYSE). Now, Nasdaq does more trading than the NYSE.

It's also hard to imagine that thirty years ago commissions were nonnegotiable. However, in 1975 Congress passed legislation that allowed brokerages to change their commission structures. The result was discount brokers like Charles Schwab and Quick and Reilly.

Internet brokers have made tremendous inroads in the financial industry. In some cases, commissions are nearly zero. Automation has made low fees possible:

There is no need to pay for expensive branches and no need to hire commissioned brokers. Rather, the new-age brokerage firm is mainly an assortment of many connected computers, all of which are hooked into advanced telecommunications networks.

ON-LINE BROKERS

THE ON-LINE DISCOUNT brokerage business's popularity has exploded. Simply put, people like making their own trades—especially at cheap prices. However, cheap prices make it difficult for discount brokers to make money. So these firms are entering new businesses such as IPOs.

Discount brokers like Schwab, E*TRADE, and DLJ have a huge number of investors and can efficiently allocate IPO shares. Because of this, these firms are able to attract major underwriters.

In fact, these discount brokers stand as real competition to traditional underwriters and there is likely to be a lowering of such fees. Perhaps this is why several investment banks have teamed up with discount brokers in offering IPOs.

DLJDIRECT

DONALDSON, LLUFKIN AND JENRETTE (DLJ) was founded in 1959 and now handles 10 percent of all trades on the New York Stock Exchange. The company has over 7,400 employees and offices around the world—including one in Moscow.

DLJ is a top underwriter of IPOs. It was ranked third by Securities Data Co. DLJ also has a well-regarded research department. Its analysts follow about 1,100 firms. The company was one of the first brokerages to go on-line. It established PC Financial Network, which is now called DLJDirect, in 1988. This division offers a full-range of discount brokerage services, including a variety of on-line research resources on the site: S&P, Lipper, Reuters, NY Times, Business Wire, TheStreet.com, and Zacks. In fact, DLJDirect even allows individual investors to get access to IPOs at the offering price.

The Resources section on page 238 lists resources for finding the latest IPOs. Select the one that looks interesting and you can download the preliminary prospectus (it can also be sent to you via mail). There is also an on-line IPO glossary to help you understand the jargon. If you want to invest, then you can fill out an on-line Indication of Interest. The DLJDirect Syndicate Department will review your request and will determine the allocation of shares.

However, there are two main requirements for participation: You must have an account with DLJ worth at least $100,000. Second, on your account form, you must indicate that your investment objective is "speculation."

E*TRADE

E*TRADE IS ONE of the fastest growing discount brokerages. The company has over 400,000 accounts and over

$10 billion in assets. About 50,000 unique visitors go the site each day. With E*TRADE, you have many investment options, such as mutual funds, index options, equity options, foreign securities and bonds. However, the commissions are still on the high end: $14.95.

Besides making trades on-line, you can place trades by Touch-Tone phone or by calling a broker.

When you surf through E*TRADE, you will find access to a lot of financial information, such as the latest IPO news from Reuters.

In September 1997, E*TRADE and the underwriter BancAmerica Robertson, Stephens and Company LLC, agreed to distribute IPOs to on-line investors. That is, for any IPO that BancAmerica Robertson, Stephens and Company is the lead underwriter, E*TRADE customers will have the possibility of getting the IPO at the offering price.

There is also access to research on industries and market development—which has been the domain of mostly institutional investors—and access to conferences, roadshows, and analysts' commentary.

E*TRADE's first on-line IPO was in December 1997. The company sold all the shares of Sportsline USA, a comprehensive sports Web site. E*TRADE investors were able to download and review the prospectus, submit indications of interest, and make purchases of the IPO—all on-line. There was four times the expected demand for the IPO stock. Of the investors eligible for purchasing the IPO, 76 percent made indications of interest for the IPO, and 56 percent participated.

Another hot IPO from E*TRADE was GeoCities, an Internet company that provides users with free Web sites. The company went public in August 1998 and soared 120 percent on the first day. However, E*TRADE does not allow you to sell the IPO for at least 30 days. If you do flip it, you are likely not to get any other IPOs in the future.

Also keep in mind that E*TRADE did not have a big

allocation of shares. In most cases, individual investors got 100 to 200 shares of GeoCities; it took less than two days to sell out the allocation.

DIGITAL STOCK MARKET

THIS VIRTUAL STOCK exchange is another innovation on which investors can trade Nasdaq and NYSE stock directly with each other. Investors will completely bypass the broker and the spreads. The spread is the difference between the bid and ask price of a stock, which goes to intermediaries known as market makers.

Institutional investors have been avoiding spreads for many years using technologies such as INSTINET. However, this trading technology is very expensive, and requires proprietary software and leased lines.

WIT CAPITAL DISCOUNT BROKERAGE

THE GOAL OF Wit Capital is to provide a one-stop shop for investors, which is why it has a discount brokerage operation. To participate, you will need a minimum investment of $1,000. To open a margin account you will need $2,000.

You can trade Nasdaq and OTC stocks for $14.95 (no limit to the size of the transaction) and up to 5,000 shares for a NYSE trade. You can also purchase mutual funds (3,800 load and no-load funds from 150 families of funds), stock options, and bonds. Besides making trades on-line, you can also do so by Touch-Tone telephone or by calling a Wit Capital representative.

You have the option of opening a variety of accounts, such as: custodian, corporate, investment club, and IRA. You can also make the following types of trades: market, limit, stop, stop limit, good-til-canceled, day, and all or none.

Wit Capital has no brokers on commission, so you will not get any high pressure. Instead Wit Capital wants to encourage long-term investing, which is particularly important for successful IPO investing.

WIT CAPITAL DIGITAL STOCK MARKET: TYPES OF TRADES

1. **Hit-or-take execution.** The computer screen lists buyers and sellers, each offering a certain amount of stock at a certain price. If you see a trade that looks good, just click your mouse and the trade is executed. There is no spread or commission.

2. **Negotiated trade.** Suppose you want to sell 1,000 shares for $25. You see someone on the Digital Stock market who is offering to buy 1,000 shares for $24. You think you might be able to negotiate something, so you click a button and go into a chat room. You can communicate with the other trader and check out the interest in buying the stock at a higher price. In many cases, the buyer and seller will find middle ground.

3. **Undisclosed orders.** Sometimes you might not want to disclose the price and volume of stock you want to buy or sell. The reason is that the disclosure may influence the market (for example, a large amount of stock being offered may drive the price down). By placing the undisclosed order, however, the computer will automatically execute your offer if there is a corresponding offer.

WIT CAPITAL:
PIONEER OF VIRTUAL IPOS

IN THE IPO MARKET, there has been resistance to the changes in technology, and there are still many elements of the "old boy network." However, the Internet is finally forcing change. In fact, on-line discount brokers are spearheading these innovations. The single most prominent player in on-line IPOs has been Andrew Klein of Wit Capital.

In 1995, a beer company, called Spring Street Brewery, a microbrewery that sells Belgian wheat beers, needed to raise money. Unfortunately, the company was too small to interest a Wall Street underwriter, and venture capitalists wanted to take too much control of the company.

So, the founder of the company, Andrew Klein, decided to sell shares of the company directly to investors. One option was to sell directly to his growing base of customers—perhaps by putting a notice of the offering on the beer bottles.

Because Klein had considerable experience in finance (he was once a securities attorney at one of the most prestigious Wall Street firms, Cravath, Swaine & Moore), he decided to take another, more sophisticated, route. He organized the prospectus and made the necessary federal and Blue Sky filings, and prepared to sell the offering over the Internet. He posted the prospectus on-line and Spring Street raised $1.6 million from 3,500 investors. Overnight he became a celebrity, as *The Wall Street Journal, New York Times,* CNBC, and many other media covered the pioneering IPO.

However, Klein did not stop with the Spring Street Brewery IPO. He recognized the need for a mechanism to buy and sell stock on the open market for companies such as Spring Street that are not on a regular stock exchange. So, he created a trading system where buyers and sellers could make their transactions commission free.

The SEC stepped in and suspended trading, but to the

surprise of many, within a few weeks, the SEC turned around and gave conditional approval of the on-line trading system. From there, Klein decided to build an on-line investment bank, called Wit Capital. It would be a place where individual investors have access to IPOs at the offering price and venture capital investments. Prior to this, such services have been provided mostly to high-net-worth individuals and institutional investors.

When Wit Capital was launched in late 1997, the press gave great fanfare. "We have a user base of 140,000 people and have, so far, done twenty-five deals," says Klein. "In fact, in one of our offerings, we got 19,000 downloads of prospectus in a 48 hour period."[14]

What's more, Wit Capital is getting bigger allocations of top IPOs from such major underwriters as Goldman Sachs. "While, at first, we got 5,000 to 10,000 shares of an IPO," says Klein, "we have now been getting 50,000 to 100,000 shares."[15]

Let's take a closer look at the process:

Wit Capital, in association with other underwriters, provides IPOs on a "first come, first served" basis. In other words, there are no special preferences on who gets these shares. You can be a billion dollar institution or an investor with an account worth $1,000; it does not matter.

To take advantage of this opportunity, you must become a member by registering (for free) personal information on the Web site. You then receive e-mail messages notifying you of the latest new issues. If you are interested in one of these offerings, you can access the preliminary prospectus on-line.

After researching the investment, you will enter a Conditional Offer to buy a certain amount of stock. These offers are not accepted until the IPO becomes effective, although, before this, you can cancel your Conditional Offer at any time. Likewise, Wit Capital can revoke your Conditional Offer at any time or reduce the number of shares, perhaps because the firm believes your position is too speculative.

The price you are quoted is known as the *red-herring price*. This is a price range established by Wit Capital. For example, it might be $15 to $19. Investors will then submit their Conditional Offers at varying prices. Suppose there are some offers at $17, but many are for $18. Wit Capital will then, with this information, establish an offering price of, say, $17.50. This price will then be the price that all investors pay when the IPO is initiated.

You can enter your Conditional Offer as a *limit order*. This means you can specify that you will buy the stock up to a particular price. This is important, because the offering price of a hot IPO can escalate very quickly.

If there is an amendment to the preliminary prospectus, Wit Capital will promptly send you the revision via e-mail. A written version will not be sent.

Keep in mind that you may not be eligible to buy the stock because of Blue Sky or foreign securities laws. If you live in a jurisdiction where the offering has not been registered, you cannot participate. However, in many cases, a Wit Capital offering is registered in all states.

Once you buy the security, you are discouraged from flipping it, that is, selling it for a quick profit. Basically, Wit Capital wants you to hold onto the stock for at least sixty days. This helps promote market stability.

If the rule is violated, you may not get priority for the next offering. Maintaining a member rating on each customer and a 5 percent transfer fee imposed on the flipped trade enforces this policy.

PRIVATE PLACEMENTS

A PRIVATE PLACEMENT is an offering of securities, done before an IPO, which is usually funded by high-net-worth individuals and institutions. These investors are known as *accredited investors*. Private placements make use of a law known as *Regulation D,* which reduces the paperwork of such offerings, so the offering need not be registered with the SEC. However, compared to IPOs, private placements tend to be very illiquid and risky.

In order to participate in Wit Capital private placements, you must fill out a form on the Web site to see if you are an accredited investor. An accredited investor is defined as someone who has a net worth of $1 million, or who had income in excess of $200,000 in the past two years ($300,000 if married) and has a reasonable expectation of doing so in the current year. Wit Capital may contact various references to ensure you are indeed an accredited investor.

As a member, you will have access to the company's private placement memorandum, which is much like a prospectus. In it, you will see such things as the risk factors, industry background, and management.

If you are eligible to purchase the private placements, you receive a user ID and password with which you can access the Web site that has a list of private placements. If you find one you want to invest in, you will fill out "Subscription Agreement." These are unconditional offers.

For every private placement, Wit Capital will perform due diligence on the company to help increase the odds of success. Also, Wit Capital will provide multimedia road show presentations to help investors.

In fact, private placements are not covered by SIPC (Securities Insurance Protection Corporation), which insures your account if your brokerage firm goes bankrupt. The IPOs and Public Venture Capital Offerings are covered by SIPC insurance.

Retail brokers have avoided selling private placement securities to clients. The reason is that, since they are difficult to sell, commissions are not likely in the short term.

Rather, it is typically regional firms that sell private placements. But, the minimum investment can be $50,000 to $100,000 or more. Wit Capital wants to change this and build a private placement network that is national in scope.

PUBLIC VENTURE CAPITAL

VENTURE CAPITAL FUNDING has typically been done through investments by high-net-worth individuals and institutions. Simply put, it was never very efficient to have individual investors participate. The Internet has changed that situation.

The first Internet VC fund was from Wit Capital, called Public Venture Capital Offerings. The first fund had about $5 million to invest in start-up companies.

Venture financing can be very lucrative. The venture firm Sequoia Capital invested $2 million in Yahoo! several years ago. The investment is now worth over $2 billion. Another example is Kleiner Perkins, which invested $5 million in Netscape. Even though the stock has fallen a great deal, the venture capital investment is still worth nearly $200 million.

Venture capital firms are usually composed of only a handful of money managers, who will seek out high-growth start-up companies. They are entrusted with millions of dollars of capital from major institutions, who are looking for high rates of returns. The compensation of the venture capital money managers is typically tied to the performance of the fund. Thus, they have a big incentive to pick the right companies.

The venture capital money managers, as described in Chapter 1, will usually provide invaluable counsel and contacts in the industry which will help the firm grow. Studies show that, on average, the best IPOs were for those companies backed by venture capitalists.

If you participate in the Wit Capital venture financing program, you will have access to the preliminary offering document, which will indicate the range of prices of the offering. There may even be a roadshow.

As with an IPO, you will submit a Conditional Offer. The shares will then be allocated on a first-come, first-served basis. Also, you can place limit orders on the allocations, but you cannot buy Public Venture Capital shares on margin.

Again, like private placements, venture funding is illiquid and risky. By contract, you are restricted from selling the shares for a period that ranges from eighteen to twenty-four months, so the companies can use the money for long-term development.

Once the companies in the Venture fund reach a specified critical mass, they will then go public or will be purchased by another company. This is how investors of the Venture Fund make money. To help reduce the risk, the Venture Fund will focus on those companies that have already secured at least one round of institutional venture financing. Other important factors it looks for are a compelling revenue model and capable management.

However, since the Public Venture fund is registered under federal and state securities laws, you do not have to be an accredited investor to participate. The minimum investment is only $500.

OTHER SERVICES OF WIT CAPITAL

THE MISSION OF Wit Capital is to build a community of individual investors. This is achieved by having Member Forums. This allows you to engage in chat sessions with other investors interested in IPOs. This can be a great source of information.

However, don't accept everything at face value. Sometimes people will post messages to promote their stock. As indicated on the Wit Capital Web site: "Do not rely on the information found in this forum. We intend that it be used as a starting point for doing independent research on various companies and investing techniques."

Wit Capital is a pioneer of virtual IPOs and on-line trading. But there are other well-established firms in this field,such as those listed earlier, that also deserve consideration.

DIRECT PUBLIC OFFERINGS

A *VIRTUAL IPO* is a company that uses an underwriter whose customers are primarily on-line. However, people often confuse virtual IPOs with DPOs (direct public offerings). A company using a DPO does not use an under-writer. Instead, the company offers stock directly to the public. In many cases, these investors are customers or friends of the company. The company, in a sense, is lever-aging its goodwill to do an IPO and avoiding the costs of hiring an underwriter.

In some cases, a DPO may be sold via the Internet, as Andrew Klein did with his Wit Beer company. He set up a Web site and sold stock in the company directly to share-holders, without an underwriter.

Small companies seeking less than $5 million in capital usually pursue DPOs. In fact, if more than $5 million is raised, you need SEC approval. In most cases, companies going the DPO route have had trouble getting financing from venture capitalists or underwriters.

Until 1995, DPOs were quite rare. In most cases when a company did a DPO, it sold its stock only to its estab-lished customers, known as an affinity group. Perhaps the best known DPO was Ben & Jerry's selling its IPO stock at its ice cream stores. The offering was announced on the bowls of ice cream.

But not all companies have such loyal affinity groups. As a result, DPOs were scarce. Then the Internet arrived and offered companies a huge, cost-effective distribution channel to sell stock directly to investors.

In 1998, 1,360 companies filed for DPOs, according to Tom Stewart-Gordon of the SCOR Report. Of these filings, 1,428 were able to raise money.[16] However, it is impossi-ble to get an average price of these DPOs, since many of them do not trade on nationally registered exchanges.

Most DPOs are filed as Regulation A or Regulation D offerings, which are exempted from registration with the SEC. But this doesn't mean that the SEC does not pay attention to DPOs. While the SEC wants to help small com-panies raise capital, the agency's purpose is nonetheless to protect investors.

SOME PROBLEMS WITH DPOS

THE SIMPLICITY OF putting up a Web page makes it enticing for companies to engage in securities fraud. And, yes, there have already been numerous cases of DPO fraud.

One such case is Interactive Products and Services, of Santa Cruz, CA. The company raised $190,000 over the Internet from 150 investors. Unfortunately for those investors, the company was a complete sham, and investors lost everything. Netcaller, the company's only product, was a figment of the founder's imagination, based on a rejected patent application. Interactive Products made false statements in its Web prospectus and the founder spent the money it raised on personal items such as clothing, stereo equipment and groceries.

Interactive Products' Netcaller was described in its prospectus as: "[A] hand-held cordless Internet appliance which enables the user to browse the World Wide Web, send and receive e-mail messages, have real-time communication through the Internet, and two-way voice communications using Internet telephone software."

Interactive Products actually did extensive Web banner advertising, many of which stated "The next Microsoft is offering its stock to the public over the Internet." When you hear such inflated claims of a product that is seemingly too good to be true, stay far away.

The SEC has established a new group called the Cyber Force, which is composed of volunteers. Essentially, they surf the Web looking at DPO sites, discussion groups, and chat areas to find evidence of fraud, pyramids and other schemes. Many of the leads that the Cyber Force gets is from the public. You can post a message to this group on the SEC Web site.

There are other concerns with DPOs, including lack of liquidity. There is usually no market for buying and selling shares in a DPO. One company, Real Goods Trading, did a DPO and allowed its investors to trade their stock from its Web site. In such cases, the transaction is then cleared through an escrow agent. But even this approach does not guarantee a good price for your stock. If you check the Web site, you will see very little trading activity. Another approach is to warn investors in the prospectus that the stock is illiquid and will need to be held for the long term. Drew Field, a renowned expert in the DPO field (who has successfully raised over $120 million for companies), believes that a DPO should "be listed on a registered national securities exchange as soon as it meets minimum numerical standards."[17]

It is not common for DPOs to be registered on national exchanges. According to Stewart-Gordon, of its DPO database, eight were listed on the Nasdaq, where fifty were on the Over-The-Counter Bulletin Board. "Most of them have taken a serious hit," says Stewart-Gordon, "as one would expect with the only people who have heard of a company are the people who want to sell their shares."[18]

Actually, liquidity really should not be a part of DPOs. Says Stewart-Gordon: "You must remember that the intent of Reg A and Rule 504 was never to create mini-big board companies. Free transferability was granted so that the investor could sell his shares if he suddenly found himself in need. The original idea behind Reg A and Rule 504 was to give the man in the street the same ground floor opportunities that venture capital companies had (this was in the days when venture capital companies were small and made seed investments). It was always assumed that the investors would hold on for three to seven years and would probably cash out when the company was sold to a larger competitor or did an IPO and became listed on an exchange."[18]

Another chief concern with DPOs is the absence of an underwriter to chaperone the deal. DPOs bypass underwriters. This means that vital tasks such as due diligence, research, and deal structuring, which ordinarily fall to underwriters, are left largely unmonitored and without expert assistance.

However, Field provides advisory services similar to that of an underwriter: pricing of the stock, distribution and marketing, filings with regulatory authorities, "corporate cleanup," changes in corporate structure, business plan development, preparation of the prospectus, and listing of the stock on an exchange.

One of Field's DPOs was the California Financial Holding Company. Founded in the depths of the Great Depression, the company decided to go public in 1983 by selling $6 million in shares to its depositors and borrowers. Fields was able to get two national brokerage firms to support trading of the stock.

Within two years the shares were trading at $30 (after adjusting for splits). In 1997 the company was acquired at $60 per share. You can see his current clients on his Web site at www.dfdpo.com.

According to Field, to find a good DPO, you are required to do your own homework. The reason is that there is no brokerage firm that is publishing research reports on the company. "Before investing in a DPO," says Field, "one should feel capable of making this analysis. This means they should stick to companies they know or are able to understand."[19]

Spin-offs

HEN A COMPANY (called the *parent*) sells all or a part of a subsidiary or division to the public, creating a new, independent company, the result is a spin-off. As a result, shareholders will have stock in two different companies. Typically spin-offs come from large corporations, such as Viacom, AT&T, or General Motors, because they have many divisions that can be split off and distributed to the public in an IPO.

Spin-offs can be very lucrative. An academic study in the 1993 *Journal of Financial Economics* shows that spin-offs beat the S&P 500 by 10 percent per year in the first three years of being independent.[20] What's more, a study from Pennsylvania State University concludes that one out of seven spin-offs are eventually taken over at a premium to its current market value.[21]

In a spin-off, the stock price of the subsidiary is based on the exchange ratio. The exchange ratio is a percentage of the current stock price of the parent company. For example, suppose that XYZ decides to spin-off its Z subsidiary. The parent determines that it will issue 0.92 (or 92 percent) shares of Z to existing shareholders. So, if the current price of XYZ is $100, you will be issued IPO shares at $92 per share in Z.

TYPES OF SPIN-OFFS

THERE ARE THREE basic types of spin-offs:

1 Traditional spin-off

2 Spin-off with equity carve-out

3 Split-off

TRADITIONAL SPIN-OFF

THE TRADITIONAL SPIN-OFF occurs when the parent company distributes 100 percent of the subsidiary to existing shareholders on a pro rata basis. Outside shareholders are not given an opportunity to get shares—that is, until the shares trade in aftermarket.

For example, if company XYZ decides to spin off the Z subsidiary, the shareholders of XYZ will get, on a pro rata basis, 100 percent of the shares of the Z subsidiary. However, the XYZ shareholders do not have to pay for these Z shares. Why? The reason is that the company is being divided into two pieces. Once this is done, the shareholders of XYZ can sell their Z stock to the general public.

SPIN-OFF WITH EQUITY CARVE-OUT

A SPIN-OFF WITH EQUITY CARVE-OUT is created when the parent distributes a minority position in a subsidiary to existing shareholders.

For example, XYZ decides to distribute 20 percent of Z to the public in an IPO. The remaining 80 percent is then distributed to existing shareholders. Why 20 percent? Because if it were more, the transaction would not be tax free. In fact, to make sure the transaction is tax free, the parent corporation needs to get a tax ruling from the IRS.

In fact, a main reason parent companies like doing carve-outs is that it raises cash by offering the IPO to the public. By issuing 20 percent of Z, the public must pay for the 20 percent, since the remaining 80 percent is owned by the parent corporation.

For example, when Lucent was spun off from AT&T in 1996, about 18 percent of the company was sold to the public, making this spin-off one of the biggest IPOs ever. Because of the size of the transaction, AT&T feared that there would be undue pressure on the price of Lucent. So, AT&T did not issue the remaining 82 percent of the share of Lucent until several months later.

SPLIT-OFF

A SPLIT-OFF HAPPENS when existing shareholders have the option to swap all or a part of their existing shares for new shares in the subsidiary based on an exchange ratio set by the parent company. In this type of transaction, there is no money raised for the parent company (since

WHY COMPANIES SPIN-OFF

◆ **Enhance shareholder value.** The main reason for spin-offs is to increase total shareholder value. In other words, management is trying to get the stock price as high as possible, which is definitely good news for investors.

◆ **Get new customers.** A prime example is Lucent. When it was part of AT&T, a variety of customers did not want to do business with the Lucent subsidiary because they were competitors of AT&T. After the spin-off, business soared for Lucent.

◆ **Unload.** Sometimes parent companies consider a subsidiary to be a non-essential (or even failing) business and want to sell it off to the public, ideally for a good price. This is a particularly popular practice when the IPO market is very strong. The parent company may even transfer debt from its balance sheet to the subsidiary. Investors beware.

◆ **Meet legal regulations.** A parent company may spin off because it is in violation of the antitrust laws. This is basically the case with AT&T, which spun off its Baby Bell companies.

◆ **Create easier valuation.** By doing a spin-off, it becomes much easier to value the parent and the subsidiary. In fact, analysts typically upgrade their evaluation of both when there is a spin-off. Example: Sears' 1993 spin off of Dean Witter-Discover and AllState.

◆ **Remove "rich uncle syndrome."** A subsidiary that is part of a major corporation can sometimes be shielded from the demands of competition. By doing a spin-off, the subsidiary will, ideally, be invigorated by participating in the market.

the company is merely being divided). A split-off is equivalent to a stock buy back. The parent corporation will attempt to make the exchange ratio attractive enough for shareholders to swap stock in the parent corporation for stock in the subsidiary. The result is that there are fewer shares of the parent company left.

FINDING GOOD SPIN-OFFS

YOU'LL SEE ANNOUNCEMENTS of company spin-offs printed in major financial publications, such as *The Wall Street Journal* and *Investors Business Daily.* However, information in these articles tends to be very sparse. Thus, you will need to investigate the company's financial data further.

After announcing a spin-off, it may take six months to a year, or even longer, for a company to make SEC disclosures. It is possible to purchase shares in the parent company before the disclosures, although, this is risky, since it is advisable to read the disclosures before investing in a spinoff. So, to play this game wisely, you need some patience.

The SEC disclosure document for a spin-off is the Form 10, which has most of the information needed to make an investment. Usually, the Form 10 will go through several amendments. So, make sure you have the latest document. The document is like a prospectus, but usually shorter.

You should also get the company's other financial statements, such as the annual reports and quarterly reports. If a spin-off represents a large percentage of the parent company, there is also the requirement to file a proxy statement, so that shareholders can vote on the transaction.

Such documents can be several hundred pages in length, but you do not have to read everything. You only need to focus on certain parts, such as:

◆ **Major stock ownership.** Make sure that management has a significant stake in the company. Ownership of 10 to 20 percent by management should be a enough of an incentive.

◆ **Pro forma financial data.** Form 10 contains pro forma income statements and balance sheets, listed as though the company were independent. Has the company done well? Are earnings and revenues growing? By being freed from the parent, is it likely that these numbers will improve?

◆ **Big name in the new company.** Look to see if a top-notch CEO will head the spin-off. When Marriott decided to spin off its hotel properties into a new entity called Host Marriott, the current CEO of Marriott, Stephen Bollenbach,

RECENT SPIN-OFFS

OF THE RECENT spin-offs, the best performing ones had strong brand names and dominant market positions. These include:

◆ **Hertz Corp.** The company operates the largest car rental business in the world, based on revenues and volume of rental transactions. When Ford did the spin-off, Hertz had generated record revenues of $3.7 billion and net income of $158.6 million. The company had been profitable since 1952. The offering price was $24 in February 1997, and the current stock price is $43.

◆ **Hartford Life.** This was the spin-off of Hartford Financial Services. Hartford Life is a leading insurance company that provides such services as annuities, retirement plans, and mutual funds to more than 15 million customers. The company is the largest writer of individual annuities and individual variables annuities. The company saw its assets grow from $23 billion in 1992 to $80 billion in 1996. The offering price was $28.25 in May 1997, and the current price is $50.

decided to become the CEO of the new Host Marriott company. He obviously saw a lot of upside to this new company. What's more, management was motivated with 20 percent of the stock. Within four months of the spin-off, the stock tripled.

◆ **Market.** There is a section in the Form 10 called "Business of the Company." Focus on how much of the market the company has. Do they have major customers? Is their market expanding?

◆ **Rationale.** It's important to read the section of Form 10 that is called "Reasons for the Distribution." Knowing why a company is choosing to spin-off can provide valuable clues for investors.

Fad
IPOs

ANIAS AND fads often drive the IPO market. It loves to highlight the next "big thing." But in the long term, fads eventually fizzle out, leaving loyal investors with huge losses.

A fad is a huge trend that sweeps the nation, if not the world. In the vein of Charles MacKay's classic book, *Extraordinary Popular Delusions and the Madness of Crowds,* sometimes people stampede to buy a product that is of questionable value. But a fad is short term, lasting, at most, several years. The masses eventually become bored and move on to something new.

This reality does not mean that you should never invest in fad IPOs. After all, you have the potential to make a lot of money very quickly. In fact, you can profit from fad IPOs even after the fad has become quite prominent.

One fad that made considerable cash for its investors

was the Home Shopping Network (HSN). The company was founded in 1977 by Lowell Paxson, who sold products on the radio. Then one day he had the bright idea of selling products on television—thus, creating a completely new retailing market. The company went public in 1986 at $18 per share. On the first day of trading, the stock soared to $42. Despite this huge increase, there was more to come. By 1987, the stock was up over 1,500 percent.

Unfortunately, the company had trouble maintaining its inventory and announced earnings that were far below what analysts were predicting. By October 1987, the stock was selling for $5.

Be cautious: the rate of return for a fad IPO will usually last a year or two. Then the consumer moves on, and the stock plunges. So, it is crucial to be very quick when investing in fad IPOs. These are definitely not buy-and-hold investments.

SPOTTING THE FADS

SOMETIMES A FAD is not a fad at all. For example, when McDonald's went public in 1965, many thought fast food was the craze of the moment and would quickly fizzle. Instead, fast food met a consumer need that has lasted over thirty years.

A more recent example is Reebok, which originally sold aerobic shoes. The company went public in 1985 and since then has made many investors rich. Even during the IPO, many thought that Reebok's fame was temporary—after all, it had all the signs of a bona fide fad. After the first year of its IPO, the company soared over 400 percent.

Fads tend to take some time to develop. For example, even though baseball cards have been in existence since the late 1800s, it took until the 1980s for baseball cards to become a full-fledged fad. Or, consider wine coolers. These fruity wine drinks were created in the mid-1970s, but did not reach fad status until the early 1980s. So the point at which a product transforms from a mere product into a consumer phenomenon is by no means a science. But, perhaps because of the proliferation of mass media, the last few decades have seen more than their share of fads.

FOCUS ON FADS

MANY FADS ENTERED the market with a novel idea, but soon witnessed their demise due to increased competition or loss of public interest. After reading their stories, you might think twice before investing in a fad IPO. They can be great money makers, but if you stay in too long, chances are the stock will depreciate.

PLANET HOLLYWOOD

ON THE FACE of it, it sounded like a winner: Sign up top tier celebrities such as Demi Moore, Bruce Willis, and Arnold Schwarzenegger to help promote a theme restau-

---

MAJOR FADS OF THE PAST TWENTY YEARS	
Cabbage Patch Dolls	Rubik's Cubes
Baseball Cards	Pet Rocks
Bagels	Wine coolers
Mighty Morphin Power Rangers	CB radios
Snapple	Beanie Babies

---

rant with a cool name, Planet Hollywood. In a short time the company was able to create tremendous brand name buzz. It became *the* place to eat as locations opened up in several major cities.

With such fanfare, the IPO performed fantastically. The offering price was $18 per share, and the company raised $200 million. The stock hit a high of $28 in 1996. Now, after two years, the stock is trading at $9 per share. As the stock price indicates, it takes more than hype and glitz to make a successful restaurant.

BAGEL MANIA

NO DOUBT ABOUT it, millions of people love to eat bagels. Several years ago, a variety of bagel companies went public. It was a mania. Ultimately, investors lost lots of money. Here are some of the nightmare stories:

◆ **Manhattan Bagel.** This company went public in June 1994, raising about $23 million. In November 1997, the company filed for bankruptcy because it could not pay its creditors. Simply put, the company was losing too much money.

◆ **Big City Bagels.** This company has also been selling lots of bagels. Unfortunately, it cannot seem to generate a profit. The company went public at $11 in August 1996. The stock is now selling for $3.

◆ **New York Bagel Enterprises.** This company went public in the summer of 1996. The company did its IPO at $9 per share and increased to $11 on its first day. The company was able to raise $15 million. The company now sells for $3.

REASONS FOR THE BURST OF THE BAGEL BUBBLE

- ◆ **Competition.** The barriers to entry are very low. Setting up a bagel shop is relatively inexpensive and, as a result, many people got into the business at once. With so many bagel shops, there was fierce price competition and not enough profits to go around.
- ◆ **Consumer sentiment.** Consumers started to realize that too many bagels are not necessarily slimming. Demand started to fall off when dieters cut back on their bagel consumption.
- ◆ **No differentiation.** For the most part, a bagel is a bagel. Does it really matter where you buy one? In other words, it became difficult for bagel shops to differentiate their product and engender customer loyalty.

◆ **Einstein-Noah Bagel.** Merrill Lynch was the underwriter. The company went public in August 1996 at $17 per share. The stock climbed to a high of $36. The current stock price is $8.

TOYS

YOU WILL OFTEN find fads in the toy business. The product life cycle for most toys is notoriously short. True, there are notable exceptions, such as Mattel's Barbie doll, which has been the all-time best-selling toy for the last thirty years.

But, for the most part, toys are essentially fads. A prime example was Coleco's Cabbage Patch dolls, which every kid seemed to want in the mid-1980s. But, as the craze died, so did the company.

Another example is Happiness Express. When the company went public in January 1995, the prospectus indicated that 82 percent of its sales derived from Mighty Morphin Power Rangers. These toys were selling like hot cakes, but the company was burning cash at a frightening rate ($10 million in nine months), and inventories were skyrocketing. All this was explained in the prospectus, but investors bought the stock anyway. When the fad ended, so did the stock. In September 1995, the company announced earnings that were below Wall Street expectations. The stock hit $5.

KNOWING WHEN TO GET OUT OF FAD IPOS

THE REAL KEY to investing in fad IPOs is knowing when to sell. Again, there is no exact science. Many fad stocks are extremely volatile and subject to periods of profit-taking. But here are some sell signals to watch for:

◆ **Mounting competition.** This is perhaps the best indicator that it's time to sell a fad IPO. Snapple, for example, did extremely well after its IPO, but it didn't take long for the major soft drink companies to enter the market. Several Snapple clones appeared on the scene at a rapid pace, quickly eating away at Snapple's market share.

The baseball card fad fizzled, too, after too many competitors tried to get in on the game. Because of the success of the original Topps baseball cards, many other companies entered the market, such as Classic, Score, Upper Deck, and Action Packed. There was a flood of baseball cards on the market and, as a result, consumers did not know which ones to buy. The market eventually collapsed, as did the stocks.

◆ **Major drop in earnings.** When analysts are shocked by a fad IPO's poor earnings report, a large drop in the stock price is probably not far behind. This is usually a good time to sell, because, in many cases, the news only gets worse.

◆ **Drop in prices.** If a company announces its plans to drop its prices, this is a major danger sign. It may mean that the company has large amounts of inventory that it cannot sell.

CHAPTER

16

Stock
Options and
IPOs

T HE PROMISE OF stock options is becoming a very common way for companies to attract talent. In fact, options are offered to employees at all levels, not only to senior management. Several secretaries at Netscape, for example, made close to a million dollars from stock options because of that hugely successful IPO.

What's more, options are a great way to motivate the work force because employees' interests are aligned with the performance of the company. Furthermore, it costs a company nothing to offer stock options. This is very financially enticing for small companies which do not have large pools of capital reserved for recruitment.

But not everyone agrees that stock options are a good thing. For example, the famed investor Warren Buffett in his Berkshire Hathaway 1997 annual report indicated that he believes stock options can be a big drain on earnings over the long-term for a company as the value of the stock gets diluted—because the company must issue more and more shares. Writes Buffett: "When Berkshire acquires an option-issuing company, we promptly substitute a cash compensation plan having an economic value equivalent to that of the previous option plan. The acquiree's true compensation cost is thereby brought out of the closet and charged, as it should be, against earnings."

Despite this, options are becoming a standard of compensation. It is not uncommon, especially in high-tech companies, for 30 to 40 percent of an employee's salary to be stock options. In fact, a CEO may have 75 percent of his or her income based on stock options. John Lauer, the CEO of the mining company Oglebay Norton, has no traditional salary at all, and instead receives all his compensation from stock options.

Even IPO advisers are taking stock options as

compensation. For example, Venture Law, a firm that has been involved in a variety of IPOs, requires that it receive stock options for every company it represents.

But stock options are extremely complicated. Interestingly enough, many senior executives have no clue how these options really work. The truth is that stock options are very risky. For example, if your company goes bankrupt, or fails to execute the IPO, your options could expire worthless.

Keep in mind that most start-ups fail within the first two years. In a sense, stock options are a type of lottery ticket. If the company takes off, you win big; if not, you lose everything.

In fact, one of the main reasons stock options have been so lucrative is the sustained bull market. But if the stock markets plunge and we enter a bear market, stock options will be far less appealing.

Before you accept any stock options, seek counsel of a good CPA or tax attorney. It will be well worth the fees to structure a deal that makes sense for you. Because of the complexity of stock option plans, it is not uncommon for an employer to offer a deal that, while on the surface looks promising, is actually quite risky.

THE BASICS OF STOCK OPTIONS

ESSENTIALLY, A STOCK OPTION gives you the right to buy a certain number of shares in a company for a specified price over a period of time (usually ten years). The exercise price is usually the current market price of the stock on the date the options were granted.

But most options have a vesting period. That is, you must hold onto them for a period of time until you can exercise them. The vesting typically begins one year after the hire date and fully vests employees after four years.

There are many potential hiccups in the vesting process. For example, suppose you decide to leave the firm and have options worth $100,000. If you are not vested, you forfeit this gain. So, pay very close attention to the vesting period of your options.

Furthermore, pay attention to what the options contract calls for when the option holder dies. For example, some contracts will terminate the options, whereas others may give the executor sixty days to exercise the options.

TYPES OF STOCK OPTIONS

EMPLOYEES WHO ARE granted stock options in a pre-IPO company have the best odds for big upside. Typically, these shares are disbursed in quantity and at a low exercise price. For example: suppose your company grants you 10,000 shares at a $1 exercise price, and the stock soars to $50 on its IPO, you now have a profit of $490,000. These returns, though rare, can be achieved nearly overnight.

There are three types of stock options: ISOs (incentive stock options), nonquals (nonqualified stock options), and restricted stock options. The difference between these is in terms of how each one is taxed.

NONQUALS

SUPPOSE YOUR EMPLOYER grants you 1,000 nonqual stock options with an exercise price of $1. Then, a year later, your company goes public and the value of the stock is $20. If you exercise your stock options and obtain 1,000 shares, you will realize a gain of $19,000. The company will report the $19,000 on your W-2 and it will be treated as ordinary income. You will then report this income on your current year's tax return. Now, suppose you sell the 1,000 shares in the open market for $20. This will be treated as a capital gain.

ISOS

AS LONG AS THE ISO options are set up properly, you will not pay any taxes when you exercise the options. That is, you do not pay taxes until you sell the shares. The increase in value is treated as a capital gain. However, there is one hitch: The gain is considered ordinary income for purposes of computing the alternative minimum tax (AMT), which applies to many high-net-worth individuals. One strategy to minimize the affect of AMT is to sell a small amount of options each year.

ISOs last for ten years (after which, they are worthless); they typically need to be exercised while you are working for the company (or within three months after you leave); you need to hold onto the option for at least two years from the date they were granted and one year after they were exercised (they can be redeemed if you die). If you do not hold onto the stock options for the two years, they become nonquals. Finally, ISOs are not transferable, cannot have an exercise price below the current value of the company's stock price, and must not be worth more than $100,000 that can be exercised in any given year (if this limit is exceeded, the options automatically become nonquals).

Note: An employer may offer a package that includes both ISOs and nonquals.

RESTRICTED STOCK

THIS IS NOT an option, but a rather a grant of stock to an employee. Also, when you receive restricted stock, you pay no taxes. But, as the name implies, there is a big restriction: you must hold onto the stock for a certain period of time (if not, you forfeit it). Companies prefer restricted stock because it keeps employees with the firm for the long term while their stake matures.

Let's look at an example: Suppose your firm offers you 1,000 shares of restricted stock. The fair market value of the company is $1 per share. You must hold onto the stock for five years. Three years later, the company goes public at $30 per share. And, after two years, the stock is selling for $100. You have a $90,000 profit. Even if you do not sell the stock, you must still pay taxes on this profit as ordinary income, since the five years have expired.

One option is to take an 83(b) election. This allows you to pay taxes on the restricted stock when you receive the grant. Then, after five years, you will owe capital gains taxes.

Of course, if you forfeit the stock, you can only claim a tax loss to the extent of what you paid for the stock—which, in many cases, is zero.

OTHER TYPES OF PRE-IPO STOCK COMPENSATION

IF YOU WORK for a private company, you may be eligible to receive stock appreciation rights (SARs). SARs entitle the holder to receive an amount equal to the excess of the fair market value of a share of common stock on the exercise of the SAR on the date of grant. A SAR can be settled in cash, common stock, or a combination of the two.

There are three types of SARs:

1 Tandem SAR. These allow you to receive the gain as either an SAR or a stock option. The exercise of one cancels the other.

2 Freestanding SAR. These are known as *phantom stock.* Here's how it works: Your employer offers you 1,000 shares of phantom stock at $10 per share. This stock is really not stock at all; rather, it moves up or down based on the market value of the company (for private companies, it is usually an appraiser who determines the market value). If the market value is $20, you will receive $10,000 in cash, which will be treated as ordinary income. You will not have to exercise your shares. It is very straightforward.

3 Additive SAR. Unlike a tandem SAR, this type of arrangement includes both a SAR payment and an exercise of an option.

NUTS-AND-BOLTS OF STOCK OPTIONS

WHEN TO SELL

ACCORDING TO A variety of academic studies, employees tend to exercise their options almost immediately because of the instant profit. But, the real value of options derives from looking to the long term. Selling your Microsoft or Oracle options on the day of the IPO would have been a definite mistake.

NEGOTIATION TIPS

NEGOTIATING YOUR STOCK OPTION compensation package can result in a much better deal. Here are some tips on what to request:

◆ Ask that the company reprice your options if they go underwater.

◆ Ask for a shorter vesting period.

◆ Ask that your options not expire worthless should you decide to leave. Also, make sure that, if your options have vested, you can exercise them when you leave. For example, a top executive of IBM sold $1 million in options one month before he left the company. The IBM contract had specified that, if an employee leaves within six months of exercising the options, he or she must forfeit the gains. The case went to litigation.

◆ Ask for the company to provide cashless exercise of your options. If they offer loans for such a purpose, ask for a low amount of interest.

◆ Ask what other persons of similar position are getting as compensation.

◆ Ask that your stock options automatically vest if the company is merged or bought out.

◆ If some of your stock options are based on your performance, make sure the performance standards are clear. For example, one might be: "Achieve 15 percent increase in sales after the first year."

WHEN TO EXERCISE

THERE ARE VARIOUS strategies on when to exercise your options. For the most part, it depends on the type of options you have:

◆ **ISOs.** Since you do not pay taxes when you exercise these options, it really does not matter when you exercise.

◆ **Nonquals.** Knowing when to exercise is very tricky. Since you must pay taxes when you exercise nonquals, many people will defer the exercise as much as possible. But, then again, if you exercise nonquals earlier, you will get capital gains treatment on subsequent transactions, which will likely be at a lower rate. You must also consider the fact that you might want to diversify your money into other investments *(see "Diversification" below)*. Also, if you believe your company will not experience much capital appreciation, it may make more sense to exercise early.

◆ **Diversification.** Suppose you have 100,000 stock options when your company goes public, reaching $40 per share. You are now worth a cool $4 million. However, suppose all other assets you own amount to $500,000. It would probably be a good idea to start diversifying into other assets. After all, even high-flying stocks can hit the skids.

Keep in mind, however, that selling your stock can be perceived negatively by company executives, who may see it as a sign that you lack faith in the firm's prospects. Nevertheless, such concerns should not interfere with good financial planning principles.

CONCLUSION

STOCK OPTIONS PRESENT many complicated decisions. It makes sense to seek out an attorney and CPA who specialize in stock options. For example, the CPA may have computer software that will run through various simulations, adjusting for taxes, holding periods, growth rates, and your current goals and financial status. An attorney will help you with the terms of the options contract and integrate the contract with your estate plan. Seeking such advice can, over the long run, save you money, time, and anxiety.

Also, keep in mind that you should take a holistic approach to compensation. Often, employees focus too much on stock options and forget that there are other important aspects, such as sign-on bonuses, perks, and vacation time.

CONCLUSION

NITIAL PUBLIC OFFERINGS are investments that truly get the blood pulsing. They are almost always exciting and risky. As with most things that have the potential for very high upside, uncertainty is an inextricable variable in the overall investment equation. As discussed previously, the words "hype" and "IPO" are often used in the same sentence. It is not uncommon to see an IPO soar 50 percent or more on the first day and then, in some cases, sink back to its beginnings in a matter of days or weeks.

If I could point to two factors that will make the biggest difference to an IPO investor, I would name patience as the most important trait, and research as the single most vital task for success.

Patience, although a virtue, is a practical matter when investing in IPOs. The first day of an offering is not always the best time to purchase an IPO, because the excitement of the offering can lead to wild price volatility. If you're looking for a long-term investment, it's possible to spare yourself from the initial roller coaster ride by simply waiting a few weeks for the price to settle down.

For example, if you had waited about a week to buy AMAZON.com, you could have purchased it below its offering price of $18, and today you would be holding a stock that has reached a high of $208 per share just a few years later. Of course, not all IPOs are as wildly successful as AMAZON, but the benefits of waiting for the speculative buying to settle can be smart for any IPO investment.

However, before you seriously consider buying an IPO, you need to do the research. Much of this book explains "doing the research," but it's important enough to re-emphasize. The best source of information on any IPO can be found in its prospectus. As discussed in Chapter 4 in detail, the prospectus is chock-full of useful information. Here is a recap of the main points to concentrate on:

1 Does the company have a strong underwriter? Be very wary of new or inexperienced underwriters.

2 Is the company engaged in a sustainable business, or is it a mere fad? If you conclude that it is a fad, you should realize that it's not a viable long-term investment. If the company's products or services are, in fact, built around a bona fide trend, the future returns can be considerable.

3 Is there venture capital money backing the company? According to academic studies, VC-backing can be very important for the success of an IPO. A VC not only provides the needed capital to the company, but also brings alliances and helps to create the strategic vision. Also, if you find that top-name VCs have invested heavily in the company, you can be confident that they've done extensive research and are satisfied with the company's chances for success.

4 What exchange is the company listed on? Look for companies that are listed on the major exchanges such as the New York Stock Exchange or Nasdaq. If the IPO is listed on a lessor one, such as Bulletin Board, be wary.

5 What is the main source of your investment research? Although the Web can be a convenient tool for researching IPOs, not all information is reliable or unbiased. Stay away from unsolicited e-mail regarding IPOs and be careful about chat rooms or anonymous brokers. See Chapter 3 and the Resources section of this book to find information resources that are consistently reliable.

6 What does the company plan to do with the money raised from the IPO? If it is using more than 50 percent of the cash to pay off large amounts of debt, it will not have as much capital to expand its operations.

7 Does the company have lawsuits pending? Legal disputes can be particularly onerous to small companies and become a threat to future success.

8 Does management have experience running a public

company? Look for an IPO with managers who have successful track records.

9 Does the company have a broad product line and a large customer base? If demand dries up for the firm's major product, the company must have other related products to focus on for future sales. Also, if a major customer goes away, are there others there to fill the void?

10 Do you understand the industry the company is part of? A familiarity with industry trends and major players can be a big advantage in forecasting future success. Whenever possible, focus on IPOs that are in sectors you know a lot about or have an interest in.

INVESTING IN IPOS is a relatively new opportunity for individual investors. With time and practice the analysis and research required will become easier and feel more familiar. Start slow and focus on the companies that you know the most about. Do the work before you invest; I assure you that it will be worth your effort.

APPENDICES, RESOURCES, GLOSSARY

APPENDIX A

THE UNDERWRITING PROCESS

AS YOU INVEST in the IPO market, you will see three types of underwriters:

1 Majors. These firms have global reach. They can easily do several billion-dollar deals in a month. They will have thousands of brokers spread across the world. For the most part, you will not get a "flaky" IPO from a major. Examples of majors include Goldman Sachs, CS First Boston, and Morgan Stanley Dean Witter.

2 Mid-size. These firms specialize in a certain industry or region. They have several hundred brokers. It is possible to find some very good prospects with mid-sized firms because they often have special knowledge about a local firm.

3 Small firm. Be wary of the very small, unknown firms. Simply put, an IPO requires numerous resources for which small firms tend to be inadequately equipped. In fact, the era of the small firm is quickly closing.

UNDERWRITING OPTIONS

THERE ARE TWO MAIN types of underwritings:

1 Firm commitment. CDNow sold 4.1 million shares to the lead underwriters for $14.88 each, raising $61,008,000. CDNow's officers and directors maintained 67.2 percent of the outstanding common stock. The underwriters, in turn, sold the 4.1 million shares to the public for $16 each. The $4,592,000 difference is the profit for the lead underwriters, which is then shared with the members of the syndicate.

It is common for underwriters to get warrants as compensation for services, too. A warrant is the right to buy stock at a certain price—which is usually at a premium to the offering price, such as 20 percent—for a specific period of time (one to five years). The warrants may account for 10 percent of the offering. For example, if the IPO has an offering price of $10 with a 20 percent premium, the underwriter gets warrants to buy 1,000,000 shares at $12.

A firm commitment offering will also usually have an overallotment option (also called *a green shoe*). This means that if there is tremendous demand for the IPO, the underwriter can issue additional shares, say, 10 to 15 percent of the total stock issued. In the case of CDNow, the lead underwriters had an overallotment of 615,000 shares.

A firm commitment offering is risky for the underwriter. If it has problems selling the issue, the firm will be left holding large amounts of stock that no one wants.

2 Best efforts. As the name implies, best efforts means the underwriter will try to sell the offering. But there is no guarantee.

You will see best-efforts offerings for small companies that have difficulty raising money. Be very careful if you are considering a best-efforts offering. After all, it should be troubling if an underwriter does not have enough faith in a company to do a firm commitment offering. Actually, the majors and mid-size firms do not engage in such best-efforts offerings. Only the small firms do.

SELF-UNDERWRITINGS

A COMPANY MAY decide to forgo the services of an underwriter. This has been happening with greater regularity as more companies are going public at earlier stages in their business cycle.

Unfortunately, there have been very few successful self-underwritten offerings. As the old saying goes: "Stock is sold, not bought." It takes a lot of effort to get an investor to buy stock in a company. So, the distribution channels of an underwriter can be extremely valuable, despite the fact the firm will garner large amounts of fees.

Investors should be very careful of any company that does its own underwriting.

APPENDIX B

ANALYZING THE FINANCIAL
STATEMENT ITEMS

THE FINANCIAL STATEMENTS contained in the final section of the prospectus are full of numbers. By using the Ratio Analysis calculations described below, you can make sense of these numbers.

LIQUIDITY RATIOS

LIQUIDITY RATIOS SHOW the ability of a company to pay its debts. The most common liquidity ratio is the *current ratio,* which is calculated as follows:

Current Ratio = Current Assets / Current Liabilities

As a general rule, you want a company that has a current ratio of 2 or higher. There may be exceptions, which makes it important to look at the current ratios of other companies in the industry.

The next liquidity ratio is the *acid-test ratio.* This uses essentially the same formula as the current ratio, except that inventories and prepaid expenses are excluded from the math. The reason for deleting them is that these types of assets are often difficult to convert into cash.

The rule-of-thumb for the acid-test ratio is 1.1.

ACTIVITY RATIOS

ACTIVITY RATIOS INDICATE the efficiency of a company to convert current assets into cash. There are three types of activity ratios:

1 Inventory ratios. This ratio shows the relationship between the amount of goods sold and inventory. This ratio is very industry specific. For the most part, a very high inventory ratio may mean that the company does not have enough product in stock. On the other hand, a very low inventory turnover ratio might mean that the company is not selling its products. In general, the higher the ratio, the better, since a company is getting cash quicker.

The ratio is calculated as follows:

Inventory Turnover = Cost of Goods Sold / Average Inventory

To compute the average inventory, make the following calculation:

(Beginning of period inventory plus end of period inventory) / 2

2 Accounts receivable ratio. This indicates how fast a company is collecting payments from customers who are on credit. The calculation is as follows:

Accounts Receivable Ratio = Net Sales / Average Net
Accounts Receivable

Strictly speaking, you should use net credit sales for the numerator. But, most financial statements do not provide such a number. Instead, you must use net sales.

As for the average net account receivables, this is as follows:

(Beginning Balance of Accounts Receivable +
the Ending Balance) / 2

The Accounts receivable ratio shows how many times the accounts receivables have been turned into cash for one year. As a rule, the higher the better, since a company gets cash quicker.

3 Days' sales ratio. This shows how efficient a company is with its receivables. The calculation is:

Days' Sales Ratio = Ending Accounts Receivable /
Average Daily Sales

To calculate average daily sales, do the following:

Net Sales / 365

PROFITABILITY RATIOS

AS THE NAME IMPLIES, profitability ratios analyze the profits of a company. The two main ratios are:

1 Return on assets. This shows the operating efficiency of a company; that is, how well the company uses its total assets. The ratio is calculated as follows:

Return on Assets = (Income before interest, taxes, and other
income) / Average Total Assets

2 Return on equity. This is a big factor for any investor. You want to make sure that management is getting the best returns possible from the equity invested in the company. The return on equity is calculated as follows:

Return on Equity = Net Income / Average Common
Stockholder's Equity

Average Common Stockholder's Equity is as follows:

Beginning Common Equity + the Ending Balance / 2

PRICE-TO-EARNINGS RATIO

PRICE-EARNINGS RATIO is computed by taking the current price of the stock and dividing it by the EPS. For example, if XYZ is selling for $30 per share, it will have a PE ratio of 30 ($30 per share times $1 EPS). This is a technique commonly used by Wall Street analysts to measure relative valuations of companies. For example, suppose other companies in XYZ's industry sell for, on average, 40 PEs. Thus, XYZ will be sell at a discount of 20 percent of the industry. This may mean the company is undervalued.

However, in many cases, IPOs do not have any earnings (these will come several years later), so doing PE ratios does not make sense.

Perhaps a better way to value the company is by the price-to-sales ratio. Let's say XYZ has sales of $20 million and the company has a market capitalization of $10,000,000. Market capitalization is derived by multiplying the number of shares outstanding by the current stock price ($30 X 1,000,000 shares outstanding). So, to get the price-to-sales ratio, we divide the market capitalization by the annual sales. In this case, the company is selling 3 times sales ($30,000,000 divided by $10,000,000 in sales). Compare this to other companies in the industry to see if XYZ is undervalued, overvalued, or fairly valued.

DEBT RATIOS

IN ITSELF, DEBT is not bad. In fact, if a company has low amounts of debt, this may indicate that the company is too conservative. Then again, high levels of debt can be very dangerous, especially if the company hits hard times and is unable to pay the interest and principal payments. The result can be bankruptcy.

The most common indicator of debt levels is the debt-to-equity ratio. It is calculated as follows:

Debt-to-Equity Ratio = Total Long-term Liabilities / Total Stockholder's Equity

RESOURCES

IN-DEPTH IPO INFORMATION

WEB SITES, ON-LINE RESOURCES, PRINT PUBLICATIONS

Alert-IPO. This is one of the cheapest IPO subscription service available. For $34.95 per year you receive weekly summaries via e-mail that detail which companies have filed for IPOs during the past week. Every day you will receive reports on each company that has filed within the past 24 to 48 hours (www.ostman.com/alert-ipo).

Bloomberg's IPO Center. Bloomberg's site offers up-to-the-minute IPO information on its Web site, including the latest listings, pricing, and links to news stories on the companies issuing the offerings. The site also includes the Bloomberg IPO Index, which measures the performance of IPO stocks during their first year (www.bloomberg.com).

CBS Marketwatch. Data Broadcasting Corporation (DBC) is a leading provider of real-time financial information and commentary. One pertinent section is the IPO Report by Darren Chervitz (www.CBS-Marketwatch.com).

Gaskins IPO Desktop. While many sites provide statistical information on IPOs, few have ratings. Francis Gaskins, an IPO expert, provides ratings on the hot and not-so-hot upcoming Internet and tech IPOs (www.gaskinsco.com).

Internet Stock Report. This is the world's most-followed Internet stock barometer, where Wall Street meets the Web, featuring ISDEX, the Internet Stock Index. Readership includes Microsoft's Bill Gates, Netscape's Marc Andreessen, and Yahoo's Jerry Yang, among others.

Steve Harmon, senior investment analyst for Mecklermedia, writes a free daily on-line column called *The Internet Stock Report*. He frequently covers the latest high-profile IPOs (www.internetnews.com or www.isdex.com).

IPOCentral.com. This is one of the best IPO sites on the

Web. It is a joint venture between Hoover's and *EDGAR Online* (www.IPOCentral.com).

IPO Data Systems. Contains a comprehensive database of IPO financial filings. Subscription fee is $15 per month or $180 per year (www.ipodata.com).

IPO Intelligence Online. Renaissance Capital Corporation of Greenwich, Connecticut, has been providing research to institutional investors since 1992. It runs the IPO Plus Aftermarket Fund. The site carries knowledgeable research and averages 2 to 3 million Web site hits a month. Free services include: breaking IPO news; IPO filings; IPO calendars, including companies expected to go public; IPO profiles that eliminate questionable or tiny IPOs; IPO commentary; a complete IPO glossary; a guide to help individual investors; IPO chat; "IPO of the Week"; lists of Best IPOs, Worst IPOs, Foreign IPOs, and Largest IPOs. Full, six-page institutional research reports can be ordered for $50 each. The site also covers open-end mutual funds, IPO Plus Aftermarket Fund (IPOSX), NAV information, top holdings, and fund news. Prospective investors can download the fund prospectus and applications (www.ipo-fund.com).

IPO Maven. The IPO Maven site is managed by Manish Shah, a widely quoted authority on the IPO market (www.ipomaven.com).

IPOMonitor.com. IPOMonitor provides a comprehensive set of services for IPO information. The subscription fee is $29 per month or $290 per year (www.IPOMonitor.com).

IPO Spotlight. The IPO Spotlight is a subscription service that can be either e-mailed to you for $30 per month or faxed at $40 per month (www.ipospotlight.com).

Red Herring. The *Red Herring* is both a magazine and an on-line publication. It covers the high-tech sector. It's a great resource for information about the hottest IPOs, and for interviews with the "movers and shakers." Plus, there's great industry analysis. A one-year subscription for the print edition is $49 (800-627-4931; www.herring.com).

Red Herring
P.O. Box 54560
Boulder, CO 80322

Upside Magazine. Again, both a magazine and on-line publication focusing on high-tech companies (888-998-7743; www.upside.com).

UPSIDE
P.O. Box 3234
Northbrook, IL 60065

EDGAR RESOURCES

EDGAR. The SEC manages the Electronic Data Gathering Analysis and Retrieval database of financial filings. You can't afford to invest in IPOs without using EDGAR's data or frequenting another site that uses EDGAR's information (www.sec.gov).

Other very useful EDGARs ites are:

EDGAROnline. Like FreeEDGAR, EdgarOnline provides real-time access to financial filings from the SEC. There is a subscription cost, but also many benefits. The subscriptions start at $9.95 per month; the fee is based on how many filings you download. There are also free services (www.edgar-online.com).

FreeEDGAR. So far, FreeEDGAR is the only company offering free, unlimited access to real-time corporate data filed with the Securities and Exchange Commission (www. freeEDGAR.com).

Smart EDGAR. Another source of real-time SEC filings, costing $29.95 per month for 15 downloads (www.smart-edgar.com).

IPO NEWSLETTERS

◆ **The IPO Insider.** An annual subscription costs $270 (800-436-1295).

Marketing & Publishing Associates
1217 St. Paul Street
Baltimore, MD 21202

◆ **The IPO Reporter.** Editor, John E. Fitzgibbon, Jr. (212-765-5311).

> 36th Floor, 1290 Sixth Avenue
> New York, NY 10104

◆ **New Issues.** A newsletter issued every month by Norman Fosback, including e-mail alerts. Annual subscription rate is $95. Free sample available upon request (800-442-9000).

> 2200 S.W. 10th Street
> Deerfield Beach, FL 33442

MUTUAL FUNDS THAT INVEST IN IPOS

◆ **The Internet Fund, Inc.** Portfolio manager, Ryan Jacob (888-FUND-WWW; www.theinternetfund.com).

> 344 Van Buren Street
> North Babylon, NY 11704-3013

◆ **Kaufman Fund.** Managers, Lawrence Auriana and Hans Utsch (212-922-0123).

> 140 E. 45th Street, 43rd Floor
> New York, NY 10017

◆ **Munder Microcap Equity Fund.** (800-239-3334).

◆ **Munder Capital Management.** Managed by Team.

> 480 Pierce Street
> Birmingham, MI 48009

◆ **Oppenheimer Enterprise Fund.** Fund Manager: Jay Tracey (888-470-0862).

> Two World Trade Center
> New York, NY 10048-0203

◆ **Renaissance Capital.** Management team, Kathleen Shelton Smith, Linda R. Killian, and William K. Smith (888-IPO-FUND).

> IPO Aftermarket Fund
> 325 Greenwich Avenue
> Greenwich, CT 06830

◆ **Robertson Stephens Microcap Growth.** Fund Managers: David J. Evans and Rainerio Reyes (800-766-3863).

> P.O. Box 419717
> Kansas City, MO 64141

GENERAL INVESTMENT RESOURCES WITH IPO COVERAGE

WEB AND PRINT RESOURCES

Barron's. A one-year subscription to the print edition of *Barron's* is $145. *Barron's* has excellent coverage of the IPO market (800-544-0422; www.barrons.com).

> Barron's
> 200 Burnett Road
> Chicopee, MA 01020

Bloomberg Personal Finance. This is a newsstand publication for savvy investors. Published by Bloomberg, the publisher of this book (888-432-5820; www.bloomberg.com).

> Bloomberg Personal Finance Magazine, Circulation Dept.
> 100 Business Park Drive
> P.O. Box 888
> Princeton, NJ 08542-0888

BusinessWeek. A one-year subscription to the printed and on-line edition costs $39.95 (888-878-5151; www.business week.com).

> Business Week
> P.O.Box 421
> Hightstown, NJ 08520

Forbes Magazine. In addition to the magazine, the Forbes.com Web site is one of the most informative and comprehensive resources for investors. Watch for articles by Penelope Patsuris, who often covers IPOs (800-888-9896; www.forbes.com).

> Forbes Subscriber Service
> P.O. Box 5471
> Harlan, IA 51593-0971

Fortune. On occasion, you will find a story on IPOs (800-862-3438; www.fortune.com).

> Fortune
> P.O. Box 60001
> Tampa, FL 33660-0001

InteractiveWeek. *InteractiveWeek* is part of the Ziff-Davis publishing empire. This Web site is chock-full of great information on high-tech and finance. Every week, Randy Whitestone writes a column—which usually covers IPOs or companies expected to file IPOs (www.interactive week.com).

Internet World. You will see an occasional story on a high-tech IPO in *Internet World.* This publication has many stories on the cutting-edge trends of the high-tech world (www.Internetworld.com).

Investor's Business Daily. An annual subscription costs $197 (800-831-2525; www.investors.com).

> Investor's Business Daily
> P.O. Box 661750
> Los Angeles, CA 90066

Motley Fool. Motley Fool is a free Web site. You will see a variety of coverage on companies that are going public (www.fool.com).

News.com. News.com is part of c/net, which is an on-line content company. This Web site focuses primarily on the high-tech sector. You will see a variety of stories on IPOs (www.news.com).

TheStreet.com. TheStreet.com is the mastermind of the outspoken James J. Cramer. The "Companies" section is where you will find analysis of IPOs—and the analysis is always strong and engaging. A subscription is $9.95 per month (www.thestreet.com).

The Wall Street Journal. The bible of all serious investors. An annual subscription costs $175. Or, you can subscribe to the on-line edition for $49 per year; $29 if you are a subscriber to the printed version (800-JOURNAL; www.wsj.com).

> Dow Jones Publications
> 84 2nd Avenue
> Chicopee, MA 01020

Wired News. This site often contains IPO covered on this Web site. And, of course, the focus is on high-tech companies (www.wired.com).

OTHER ON-LINE RESOURCES FOR INVESTORS

Go2Net	www.go2net.com
Investor Guide	www.investorguide.com
The New York Times	www.nytimes.com
Silicon Investor	www.techstocks.com
StockSite	www.StockSite.com
Upside	www.upside.com

CHAT ROOMS AND DISCUSSION GROUPS

The Motley Fool	www.fool.com
Raging Bull	www.ragingbull.com
Silicon Investor	www.techstocks.com
Stock Chat	www.stockchat.com
Stock Club	www.stockclub.com
Stockmaster	www.stockmaster.com
Stock-Talk	www.stocktalk.com
Yahoo! Finance	www.quote.yahoo.com

INVESTMENT CLUBS

AN INVESTMENT CLUB can be a good resource of information and education. According to the National Association of Investors Corporation (NSIC), investment clubs have consistently outperformed the general market. A club will usually meet, say, once a month and cover a new topic each time. One topic could be IPOs. Sometimes a club will also invite guest speakers (810-583-6242).

To get further information on investment clubs, you can contact the NSIC at:

> 711 West Thirteen Mile Road
> Madison Heights, MI 48071

NOTES

CHAPTER 2

1 Larrie A. Weil, telephone conversations with the author, May 1998.

CHAPTER 4

2 Mark Spitzer, e-mail interview by author, July 1998.

CHAPTER 6

3 Steve Harmon, e-mail interview by author, May 1998.

CHAPTER 7

4 Harmon.

CHAPTER 8

5 Nadine Wong, e-mail interview by author, June 1998.

6 Wong.

7 Wong.

8 Wong.

9 Wong.

CHAPTER 12

10 Linda Killian, e-mail interview by author, May 1998.

11 Killian.

12 Killian.

13 Killian.

CHAPTER 13

14 Andrew D. Klein.

15 Klein.

16 Tom Stewart-Gordon, e-mail interview by author, July 1998.

17 Drew Field, e-mail interview by author, July 1998.

18 Stewart-Gordon.

19 Field.

CHAPTER 14

20 Patrick J. Cusatis, James A Miles, and J. Randall Woolridge, "Restructuring Through Spinoffs," *Journal of Financial Economics* (Spring, 1993): 105-169.

21 Cusatis, Miles and Wooldridge.

GLOSSARY

Absorbed. The condition of an IPO that has been sold out.

Accounts payable. The money a company owes to its creditors, such as, for raw materials, inventory, equipment, services, and taxes.

Accounts receivable. Money owed to a company from customers. The amount increasing much more than sales may indicate that the company is having problems collecting from its sales.

Accredited investor. A person who has a net worth of at least $1 million or has an annual income of $200,000 per year. These guidelines are set by federal regulations. It is typically accredited investors who put money into companies that have yet to go public. Because of the high income requirements, many individual investors do not participate in pre-IPO investments.

Agreement among underwriters. A document expressing the number of shares to be allocated among the comanagers and syndicate underwriters and enumerating the compensation breakdown.

Allotment. The amount of IPO stock allocated to each underwriter.

American depository receipt (ADR). A foreign company traded on a U.S. stock exchange. In most cases, ADRs are major companies.

Aftermarket performance. An indication of how well stock has performed after it has gone public. The gain or loss is measured against the offering price.

All or none. A condition providing that if a minimum amount of capital is not raised, an underwriter can cancel the offering. This is usually the case with best-effort offerings, not firm commitment offerings.

Analyst. A person who researches companies in a certain industry. Analysts work for brokerages, banks, underwriters, or other financial institutions. Because typical IPOs are small, usually only a few analysts cover an IPO company.

Arbitration. A process in which two opposing sides resolve a dispute instead of going to court. Most brokerage accounts require arbitration.

Balance sheet. A list of assets, liabilities, and equity of a company at a certain point in time. The balance sheet is included in a company's prospectus and is a valuable tool for analysis.

Bedbug letter. A notification sent by the SEC to a company to withdraw the IPO offering because the registration statement is not in accordance with the securities laws.

Best-efforts offering. An agreement stating that an underwriter will use its best efforts to sell shares of a company to the public. Thus, there is no guarantee of a minimum amount of capital for the issuer. Small companies normally use best-effort underwriters.

Blank check offering. An IPO that has yet to indicate the type of business it will enter. This kind of IPO is extremely risky.

Block. A large amount of stock—10,000 shares or more. Institutions will purchase IPOs in blocks.

Blue sky laws. State regulations for IPOs.

Book. Information maintained by an underwriter to track all buy and sell orders for a public offering.

Bought deal. *See* Firm Commitment.

Break issue. An IPO that falls below the offering price.

Bridge financing. A loan to a company in anticipation of an IPO. Part of the proceeds of the IPO will then be used to pay off the bridge loan. This is a relatively common practice.

Calendar. *See* Pipeline.

Capitalization. The amount of equity and debt a company has.

Cheap stock. Common stock issued to certain persons—usually executives and other employees—at prices much lower than what the public will pay.

Classified stock. Types of stock, such as Class A and Class B. The former will have voting rights (which is retained by the founders of the company) and the latter will be issued to the public.

Collar. The lowest price acceptable for an issuer for an IPO.

Commissions. The biggest expense for an IPO. The commissions are what the underwriters and stockbrokers make from the IPO.

Completion. The completion of all IPO trades, which takes about five days after the start of trading. Before completion, an IPO can be canceled and the moneys returned to investors.

Comfort letter. A letter from an independent auditor that indicates that the disclosures in the registration statement are correct.

Confirm. Correspondence sent to a client that gives details about a trade, such as the quantity, name of the security, price, and commission.

Cooling off period. The period of time between the filing of a preliminary prospectus with the Securities and Exchange Commission and the offering of stock to the public.

Current assets. Corporate assets such as cash, government bonds, accounts receivables, and inventory, which can be converted into cash in a year or less. Thus, current assets are an indicator of the liquidity of a company. After an IPO, a company will usually have a high amount of current assets, because of the large infusion of cash from the offering.

Current liabilities. Corporate liabilities such as accounts payable, wages, taxes owed, or interest payments, all of which come due within a year or less.

Current ratio. A company's current assets divided by its current liabilities. As a general rule, a current ratio of 2:1 shows that a company can meet its debts.

Date of issue. The date upon which an IPO begins trading on the open market.

Deal flow. The frequency at which an underwriter brings companies public.

Dilution. The weaker equity value of the IPO stock compared to that of earlier company shares, due to the increase in both the number of shares and in the cost per share.

Direct public offering (DPO). Selling directly to the public without using an underwriter, a frequent practice of small companies that have difficulty raising capital. The success rate of DPOs has not been good; although, the Internet might change that situation. A major problem with DPOs is lack of liquidity (that is, difficulty selling shares at a good price).

Discount broker. A brokerage firm that gives investors low commission rates. However, a discount broker will typically not provide any investment advice. Recently, discount brokers have been offering their clients the opportunity to invest in IPOs.

Discretionary account. The right of a broker to make transactions in a client account without authorization. This requires a signed power of attorney.

Dividend. A cash payment paid to shareholders—usually on a quarterly basis. However, since IPOs are usually small, dividends may not accrue.

Due diligence. An investigation of an issuer by the underwriter to determine the value of the company.

Eating stock. An underwriter buying IPO stock for its own account, because there is not enough demand in the open market. This is a very bad sign for an IPO.

EDGAR. A comprehensive collection of the filings from public companies. There are also prospectuses on EDGAR. You can access the site (edgar-online.com) for free. This is an extremely valuable tool for IPO analysis.

Effective date. The date on which the Securities and Exchange Commission allows a company to issue its shares to the public.

Elephant. A large institutional investor.

Financial statements. The balance sheet, income statement, and statement of cash flows for a company, all of which are disclosed in the prospectus.

Firm commitment offering. An underwriter writing a check to the issuer for a specified number of shares. The underwriter expects to sell these shares to the public at a higher price, thus generating a profit.

Flipping. Investors taking a quick profit when an IPO's value increases on the start of trading. Underwriters do not like flipping, since it places heavy selling pressure on the stock price.

Float. The number of shares that the general public owns. Float does not include the stock the insiders own.

Flotation cost. The cost of issuing new stock to the public.

Full-service broker. The traditional stockbroker, who provides financial advice but charges much higher fees than discount brokers. In most cases, it is full-service brokers who sell IPOs, although, that situation is changing.

Fully distributed. An IPO having been fully sold to the public.

Going public. *See* Initial public offering.

Greenshoe (also known as an *overallotment option*). An agreement allowing an underwriter to increase the number of shares issued on an IPO. The typical amount is 15 percent of the amount of the issue. A greenshoe option is usually included when an IPO generates high demand.

Group sales. Block sales to institutional investors.

Hot issue. An IPO that trades at a substantial premium on the offering.

House of issue. *See* Lead underwriter.

Income statement. A document showing a company's revenues and expenses. An income statement shows profits or losses and is a required disclosure in a company's prospectus.

Indications of interest (IOI). A statement from an investor indicating how many shares he or she will buy of an offering. An underwriter will collect the IOIs and determine the demand for the offering to set an appropriate price and the number of shares to be issued.

Initial public offering (IPO). A company selling stock to the public for the first time. Money from the offering can either go into the company or pay off existing share-holders—or a combination of the two.

Insider. A person who is either an officer, director, or owner of 10 percent or more of the stock of a company. In terms of an IPO, there are a variety of restrictions on how much stock an insider can sell.

Institutional investor. A firm that trades substantial amounts of stocks and other investments. Institutions include mutual funds, pensions, banks, and insurance companies.

Investment banker. *See* Underwriter.

Issue. The stock sold by a company in an IPO.

Issuer. The company that is doing an IPO.

Lead underwriter (also known as a *lead manager*). An investment bank, such as Goldman Sachs or CS First Boston, that determines the price of an IPO and how many shares should be allocated to members of the underwriting syndicate.

Liquidity. The ability to turn an asset (such as a stock) into cash quickly without suffering any loss of real value. For small IPOs, there may not be much liquidity.

Lock-up period. The 180 days after a company goes public during which the officers and insiders are restricted from selling stock.

Managing underwriter. *See* Lead underwriter.

Market makers. Professionals who buy and sell stock for their own accounts and make profits on the difference between their purchase and the selling price (called the *mark-up*). Strong market makers are crucial for an IPO. After the IPO, the market makers will provide liquidity for investors to buy and sell the issue.

Mutual fund. A pool of capital with which money managers invest in stocks and bonds. Investors can purchase shares in the mutual fund. The biggest buyers of IPOs are mutual funds.

NASD (National Association of Securities Dealers). A self-regulatory agency for the securities industry. The NASD tries to ensure fair compensation and trading practices for brokers and underwriters.

Nasdaq (National Association of Securities Dealers Automated Question System; also called the *National Market System*). A stock exchange that does not have a physical trading floor. Rather, the Nasdaq trading system is a huge network of phones and computers. Most of the companies that go public will be listed on the Nasdaq exchange.

Net income. The difference between a company's revenues and expenses. If there is a gain, the company has a net profit; if there is a loss, the company has a net loss.

New issue. *See* Initial public offering.

Offering. *See* Initial public offering.

Offering circular. *See* Prospectus.

Offering date. The date of the IPO.

Offering price. The price that the lead underwriter determines for an IPO. It is the offering price that the original investors get (usually, it is high-net-worth individuals and institutions who can buy at the offering price).

Opening price (also known as the *first trade price*). The price at which an IPO starts trading on the open market. In many cases, the price will be at a premium to the offering price.

Oversubscribed. When an IPO has more buyers than there are shares. Most offerings will have a *greenshoe option,* which will allow the underwriter to increase the number of shares of the offering if it is oversubscribed. An oversubscribed offering is a good sign and typically means the IPO will trade at a premium on the opening.

Penalty bid. A fee charged by an underwriter if investors flip an issue. That is, a penalty bid is meant to curtail flipping, a practice which can put pressure on the stock price.

Pink Sheets. Companies too small to be listed on Nasdaq. It is the National Quotation Bureau that publishes the stock quotes of Pink Sheets. The Pink Sheets market tends to be a very illiquid market.

Pipeline. Companies that have filed to do an IPO but have yet to trade.

Preferred stock. Equity in a company whose owners get dividends before common stockholders, as well as preference in the event of liquidation because of bankruptcy. But an IPO is usually not in the form of preferred stock, but of common stock. Rather, preferred stock is normally issued to venture capitalists before a stock is offered to the public.

Preliminary prospectus. *See* Red herring.

Premium (also known as *pop*). The difference between the offering price and opening price of an IPO.

Private placement. The sale of stock or debt to raise money for a company. However, the securities are not sold to the public, but instead to high-net-worth investors and institutions.

Prospectus. A document filed with the Securities and Exchange Commission for companies that want to do an IPO. The prospectus is for investors and discloses all material information, such as risk factors, financial data, management, use of proceeds, and strategies.

Public offering. *See* Initial public offering.

Public offering price. *See* Offering price.

Quiet period. The period after a company files its S-1 registration statement, during which management is not allowed to make any statements that are not included in the prospectus. The purpose of the quiet period is to prevent the "hyping" of the IPO. The quiet period lasts until twenty-five days after the stock starts trading.

Real estate investment trust (REIT). A company that invests in real estate properties. If the REIT meets certain federal requirements, it can take advantage of a variety of tax exclusions.

Red herring (also known as the *preliminary prospectus*). A document filed with the Securities and Exchange Commission before the completed prospectus is filed. This is called a *red herring* because the front page is in red ink and indicates that certain information (such as the number of shares to be issued and the price) is subject to change.

Registration statement. A document consisting of the prospectus (which is available to the public) and a statement for additional information (which is only for the SEC), all of which is filed with the SEC. Different types of registration statements include an S-1 and an SB-2.

Regulation A offering. A stock offering for a small company. The maximum amount that can be raised is $5 million. Some companies use the Internet to do Regulation A offerings, but the success rate of these has been low.

Restricted stock. Stock granted to executives, employees, and private investors of the company before the company goes public. This stock is not registered with the SEC and must comply with a variety of regulations. Typically, this stock cannot be sold until two years after it has been granted.

Roadshow. Visits of senior management to a variety of brokerages to give a presentation to potential investors. Typically, the roadshows will be in the major investment centers, such as New York, San Francisco, and Los Angeles.

SEC. *See* Securities and Exchange Commission.

Securities Act of 1933. The law that covers the regulations for the IPO market.

Secondary offering. A stock issue after a company has already done an IPO.

Securities and Exchange Commission (SEC). The federal agency that regulates securities such as IPOs and insider trading.

Self-underwriting. A company bypassing the use of an underwriter and doing its own offering. Small companies frequently underwrite themselves with the size of the offering, in most case, below $5 million. However, the success of these types of offerings has been spotty.

Selling stockholders. The officers or founders of an IPO company selling some or all of their positions. Heavy selling may indicate the IPO will not do well.

S-1. A document filed with the Securities and Exchange Commission. The filing includes the prospectus, which is also known as the *registration statement.*

Spinning. A controversial practice, in which underwriters will give certain high-level officers stock in "hot" IPOs, to potentially get future underwriting business.

Spin off. A subsidiary of a company becoming a separate company via a new stock offering. The stock is usually issued to existing shareholders of the parent company.

Stabilization. A lead underwriter intervening into the market by buying shares to prevent the stock from falling below its public offering price. This practice protects the stock, and is, therefore, allowed by the SEC.

Sticky deal. An IPO that will be difficult to sell.

Syndicate. A group of underwriters who will sell the offering to investors. IPOs are typically very large, requiring numerous underwriters. The syndicate is headed by the lead manager.

Tombstone. An advertisement for an IPO placed by the lead underwriter.

Underwriter. A firm that helps companies do an IPO.

Use of proceeds. A section in a company's prospectus that indicates what it will do with the money from an IPO.

Venture capital (known as *VCs*). Cash from firms accepted before a company goes public. The venture capital firms will usually take a large position in the company.

Waiting period. The period of time between the filing of the registration statement and the time when the shares can be offered to the public.

INDEX

accounts receivable ratio, 235
accredited investors, 190–91
acid-test ratio, 234
activity ratios, 234–36
additive SAR, 221
Alert-IPO, 54–55
AllState, 203
AMAZON.com, 22, 96, 109, 110, 116, 227
American Depository Receipt (ADR), 162
Amgen, 127, 128, 130
analysts, 97–98
angels, 21, 74
AOL.com, 116
Apple Computer, 16–17
Argentina, 161
ASD Group Inc., 85
Aspect Technology, 119
assets, 76–77
AT&T, 202, 203
attorneys, 23
auditors, 22–23
Auriana, Lawrence, 178
AutoEnhancer/2000, 83

balance sheet, 76–77
BancAmerica Robertson, Stephens and Company LLC, 185
banking, 137–40
Barron's, 49
Ben & Jerry's, 194
best-efforts offering, 88, 233
Bexxar, 132
Biacore International (BCORY), 130
Big City Bagels, 211
bioinformatics, 129
biotech IPOs, 120–32
BioTech Navigator, 123, 132
Biotechnology-Health Stock Newsletter, 132
black market, 165–66
Blockbuster Video, 152
Bloomberg Financial Markets, 51
Bloomberg IPO Index, 51
blue sky laws, 32
Bollenbach, Stephen, 204–5
Boston Market, 154
brand recognition, 145–46, 152–53
Brav, Alon, 21
Brazil, 159–60
Brilliance China Automotive Company, 165
Broadcast.com, 3, 99, 114
Broadcom (BRCM), 117, 118

brokerages/brokers, 60, 142–44
　on-line, 183–86
Buffett, Warren, 94, 145, 216–17
Bulletin Board, 39, 228
buying on margin, 102–3
Byron, Christopher, 50

Calculation of Registration Fee table, 67–68
California Financial Holding Company, 197
California Technology Stock Letter, 132
capital gains taxes, 176, 178, 220–21, 222–23
CBS Marketwatch-DBCC, 55
CDNow, 20, 22, 25, 116, 232, 233
CD Warehouse, 151, 154
Celerity Systems, 87–88
Center Watch, 130–31
Charles Schwab, 142, 143, 166, 182, 183
Chase Bank, 100
chat rooms/discussion groups, 60, 243–44
Chervitz, Darren, 55
Chile, 166
Cisco, 110, 114
cold calls, 61
comment letters, 36
commissions, 182–83
competition, 89–90, 212, 213
Conditional Offer, 189–90, 192
conflicts of interest, 74, 166–67
contract research organizations, 130
Coulter Pharmaceutical (CLTR), 132
covering a short position, 101
Cramer, James J., 49
current ratio, 234
Cyber Force, 195

days' sales ratio, 235–36
Dean Witter-Discover, 203
debt ratios, 237
Dell, 110, 114
dilution, 72
direct public offerings, 193–97
disclaimer, 68, 69
disclosure document, 204
dividends, 71, 176
DLJdirect, 184
Doerr, John, 49
Donaldson, Lufkin & Jenrette (DLJ), 183, 184
DoubleClick (DCLK), 16, 17, 115
dry laboratories, 129
Duane Reade, 151, 152, 153
due diligence, 32, 191
Dyson, Esther, 49

Earthweb.com, 3, 5, 114
eBay.com, 2–3, 5, 114
EDGAR, 48, 56–59, 240
EDGAR Online, 51, 58–59
effective date, 40
Egghead Computer, 114
83(b) election, 220–21
Einstein-Noah Bagel, 212
Ellison, Lawrence, 17
Epogen, 127
equity, 78
E*TRADE, 5, 143–44, 183, 184–86
Eudora, 111
Evans, Dale, 179
Excel Add-In, 58
exchange ratio, 200–1
Excite, 50, 116

fad IPOs, 154, 206–13, 228
Federated Investors, 141
Feshbach Brothers, 101
Fidelity, 8, 141–42
Field, Drew, 196–97
Filo, David, 18
finalization of offering, 39–40
finance services IPOs, 134–46. *See also* banking; brokerages/brokers; insurance
  company IPOs; mutual funds
financial printers, 23–24
financial statements, 74–79, 234–37
firm commitment, 232–33
flipping, 5, 98, 190
foreign IPOs, 156–67, 173
Form 10, 204–5
form S-1, 34, 57
form SB, 34, 57
Fosback, Norman, 59
franchising, 138, 154
FreeEDGAR, 58, 72
freestanding SAR, 221
front-running, 167

Gates, Bill, 49, 112
Gateway, 110
generally accepted accounting principles (GAAP), 22, 73
Genzyme, 130
GeoCities, 3, 5, 185, 186
Georgia Institute of Technology, 115
Going Public, 59
Goldman Sachs, 24
Gompers, Paul, 21
goodwill, 77

Hampshire Securities, 88
Happiness Express, 212–13
Harmon, Steve, 49, 99, 112, 114–15
Hartford Life, 145, 205
Heartland Small-Cap Contrarian Fund 94
hedging, 163
Helsinki Stock Exchange page, 166
Hertz Corp., 38, 205
Home Depot, 96, 150
Home Shopping Network (HSN), 209
Hoover's, 51
Hoover's Company Profile, 52
Horizon Pharmacies Inc., 153
Host Marriott, 204–5
Human Genome Project, 124–25, 129

incentive stock options (ISOs), 219–20, 222
income statement, 75–76
income taxes, 75, 77–78
incorporation, 69–70
Incyte, 129
INSTINET, 186
insurance company IPOs, 145–46
Intel, 108, 110
Interactive Products and Services, 195
International Data Corporation (IDC), 115–16
Internet companies, 2–3, 4–5, 86–87, 109, 114–16. *See also* direct public offerings; virtual IPOs
Internet Explorer, 112
Internet Scanner, 16
Internet Services Systems (ISS), 3, 16, 17, 67–68, 69
"Internet Stock Report, The," 49
inventory ratios, 234–35
investment clubs, 244
Investment Company Institute, 140
investment strategies, 92–103
IPOCentral, 51–52, 64
IPO Data Systems, 53–54
IPO Maven, 56
IPO Monitor, 53
IPO Plus Aftermarket Fund (IPO Fund), 172–75, 177–78
IPO Reporter, 59
IPO Spotlight, 55
Israel, 163

Jenna Lane, 84
Johnson, Walter E., 139

Kaplan, Stanley, 84
Kaufman Fund, 178
Keebler Foods (KBL), 17
Kennedy, Joseph, 100
Kerins, Patrick, 20
Killian, Linda R., 173–74, 177–78
Klaus, Christopher, 16, 17

Klein, Andrew, 187–89, 194
Kleiner Perkins, 192
Korea, 167
Lauer, John, 217
laws on IPOs, 31–32
legal proceedings, 70, 84, 228
letter of intent, 32–34
LHS Group, 112, 113
liabilities, 77–78
limit order, 190
Liposome (LIPO), 127
liquidity, 17–18, 72, 163–64, 192–93, 195–96
liquidity ratios, 234
Livermore, Jesse, 100
loads, 175
loan default
    in foreign IPOs, 163
    history of, 70, 90–91
lock-up period, 74, 98–99
Lucent Technologies, 117, 202, 203
Lynch, Peter, 94, 141–42, 155

McCamant, James, 132
McDonald's, 154, 210
MacKay, Charles, 208
majors, 232
management, 228–29
    of biotech IPOs, 131
    inexperienced, 70, 82–83
    of mutual funds, 174–75
    prospectus on, 73
    of technology IPOs, 112
management fee, 175
Manhattan Bagel, 211
margins, 130
    negative gross, 70, 86
Marine Management Systems, 90–91
market and customer base, 84–85, 229
Mecklermedia, 49, 99, 112
Medical Technology Stock Letter, 132
Meltzer, Alan, 20
mergers and acquisitions (consolidation), 137–38, 152
Mexico, 163
Microsoft, 5, 16, 17, 89–90, 109, 110, 112, 113, 116, 221
mid-size firms, 232
Mighty Morphin Power Rangers, 212–13
Minkow, Barry, 101
Molecular Dynamics (MDYN), 130
Moore's Law, 108–9
Morgan Stanley, Dean Witter, Discover, 33
Motley Fool, 50
Motorola, 124
Mullins, Jerry, 132
Munder Microcap Equity Fund, 179
Murphy, Michael, 132
Murrieta, Luis Donaldo Colosio, 163
mutual funds, 8, 97, 140–42, 170–79, 241

advantages of, 174–75
fees in, 175
investment strategies for, 176–77

Nacchio, Joseph, 118
Nasdaq, 182, 186, 196, 228
Nasdaq NM, 38–39
Nasdaq Small Cap, 39
Nasgovitz, William, 94
National Association of Securities Dealers (NASD), 35
nationalization, 163
NationsBanc Montgomery Securities, 83
Nationwide Financial Services, 145
Netcaller, 195
Netscape, 89–90, 111, 114, 192, 216
Neupogen, 127
New Issues, 59
newsletters, 59, 240
New York Bagel Enterprises, 211
New York Stock Exchange (NYSE), 38, 39, 182, 186, 228
nonqualified stock options (nonquals), 219, 222–23

Oakley IPO, 4
O'Connor, Kevin, 16, 17
Octopus Technologies, 91
offering price, 40, 98–99
offshore incorporations, 70
Oglebay Norton, 217
Olim, Jason and Matthew, 20
Omidyar, Pierre, 2–3
Onsale.com, 102, 116
Oppenheimer Enterprise, 179
Oracle, 7, 17, 221
over-allotment option (green shoe), 68, 233
over-the-counter (OTC) markets, 38–39, 196

Parexel (PRXL), 130
Paxson, Lowell, 209
penny stock, 39, 70–71, 90
Peregrine, 112, 113
Peritus Software Services, 82–83
Perseptive Biosystems (PBIO), 130
Pink Sheets, 39
plain English rules, 66
Planet Hollywood, 4, 210–11
portals, 116
portfolio managers, 141–42, 177
Preview Travel, 116
Prial, Dunstan, 48
price of issue, 33–34, 70–71, 90
price-to-earnings ratio, 236–37
price-to-sales ratio, 237
private placements, 190–91
privatization, 159, 160
product concentration, 70, 84–85, 229

profitability ratios, 236
prospectus, 19–21, 34, 62–79, 176, 227–29
protectionism, 161
proxy statement, 176–77, 204
public relations firms, 24
Public Venture Capital Offerings, 191, 192–93

Qualcomm, 111
Qualix Group, 91
Quick & Reilly, 142, 182
quiet period, 37–38
Qwest Communications (QWST), 117, 118

RCA stock, 100
Real Goods Trading, 195
RealNetworks, 18, 19, 111–12
red herring, 14, 36–37, 64
Red Herring **magazine**, 50
red-herring price, 190
Reebok, 210
Reeves, Scott, 49
Regan, John, 20
registrars, 24–25
registration statement, 34–36
Regulation A, 194, 196
Regulation D, 190–91, 194
Renaissance Capital, 55, 172
research and development (R&D), 110
resources, 48–61, 238–45
    unreliable, 60–61
restricted stock, 220–21
retail sector IPOs, 148–55
return on assets, 236
return on equity, 236
risk factors, 70–71, 80–91
road show, 36, 191
Robertson Stephens Microcap Growth, 179
Rockwell Medical Technologies (RMTI), 86
Russia, 164–65

sales per square foot, 152
Scoop, 118
Sears, 203
Securities Act of 1933 (Truth in Securities Act), 31
Securities and Exchange Commission (SEC), 22, 23, 24, 31, 34, 35–36, 66, 68,
    69, 84, 85. *See also* EDGAR
    approval granted by, 39–40
    direct public offerings and, 194, 195
    foreign IPOs and, 164
    offshore incorporations and, 70
    private placements and, 191
    spin-offs and, 204
Securities Exchange Act of 1934, 31
self-underwritings, 233
semiconductors, 129

Sequoia Capital, 192
Shah, Manish, 55
ShareData, 144
Shopping.com, 84
short selling, 99–102
Silicon Investor, 50
Singapore, 161
SkyMall, 87
small firms, 232
Smith, Kathleen and William 174
Smith, O. Bruton, 153
software companies, 112, 113–14
Sonic Automotive, 153
Soros, George, 100
Southwest Bancorporation of Texas, Inc., 139
Southwest Securities, 40
spam, 60–61
spinning, 34
spin-offs, 198–205
   with equity carve-out, 202
   split-off, 202–3
   traditional, 201–2
Spitzer, Mark, 72
SportsLine USA, 115, 116, 185
S&P Personal Wealth Service, 50
Spring Street Brewery, 187–88
Starbucks, 150, 153
Steinhart, Michael, 100
Stewart-Gordon, Tom, 194, 196
Stock Appreciation Rights (SARs), 221
stock as currency, 18
stock exchanges   digital, 186
   listed, 38–39, 228
***Stock Market Logic* (Fosback)**, 59
stock options, 8, 16, 214–23
Stocksite, 50
Subscription Agreement, 191

tandem SAR, 221
technology IPOs, 106–19. *See also* Internet companies; software companies;
   telecommunications
technology risk, 85–86
Telebras, 159–60
telecommunications, 117–18, 159–60
theglobe.com, 3
ThermaCell Technologies, 88–89
TheStreet.com, 49–50
TicketMaster-CitySearch, 3, 5
tombstone ads, 37–38
toys, 212–13
Tracey, Jay, 179
transfer agents, 24–25
Turkey, 158
12b-1 fee, 175

uBid.com, 3, 5
underwriters, 25–26, 32–34, 74, 84, 194, 228
underwriter's discount, 18
underwriting process, 232–33
Union Pacific Railroad stock, 100
unsolicited mail, 61
U.S. Steel, 7
USN Communications, 118
Utsch, Hans, 178

venture capital, 21–22, 74, 192–93, 228
Venture Law, 218
Ventus, 127
VeriSign 3, 33, 116
vesting period, 218–19, 222
virtual IPOs, 180–93. *See also* direct public offerings; Wit Capital
Vivo, 18

Waddell & Reed Financial Inc., 141
Wall Street Journal, 48–49
Wal-Mart, 96, 150, 151
Walton, Sam, 151
warrants, 232–33
Watchlist, 58
Web sites. *See also* resources
    biotech company, 130–31
    company, 60
    for foreign IPO information, 166
Weill, Larrie, 40
wet laboratories, 129
Wiggan, Albert, 100
Wilmut, Ian, 122
***Wired* magazine**, 23–24
Wit Capital, 5, 36, 186–93, 194
Wong, Nadine, 123–24, 125, 130, 131, 132
Wong, Scott, 132
WorldCom, 160

Yahoo!, 18, 50, 109, 116, 192
Yang, Jerry, 18, 49
Year 2000 Problem (Y2K), 83, 85–86

ZZZZ Best, 101

ABOUT THE AUTHOR

Tom Taulli is an expert in the IPO field and appears regularly on CNN and CNBC. He has written about the stock market for a variety of publications including *Barron's, Research Magazine,* and *Registered Representative.* He also writes columns on IPOs for such on-line publications as *Microsoft Investor, TechInvestor,* and *StockSite.* Tom Taulli is the founder of WebIPO, a pioneering on-line investment banking company. He also helped develop IPO Monitor, an on-line source of IPO information. He's an often-quoted source in IPO stories, most recently in *Barron's, The Economist, Forbes,* and TheStreet.com. The author has his own financial Web site at **WWW.TAULLI.COM.**